Step-by-Step Guides

Microsoft Works

Richard Thomas MSc, BSc(Hons), Cert Ed
Southampton Institute Management Centre

Stanley Thornes (Publishers) Ltd

First published in 1992 by:
Stanley Thornes (Publishers) Ltd
Ellenborough House
Wellington Street
CHELTENHAM GL50 1YD
United Kingdom

Reprinted 1993
Reprinted 1994
Reprinted 1995

A catalogue record for this book
is available from the British Library.

ISBN 0-7487-1394-8

Titles in the Step-by-Step Series:

WordPerfect 6
WordPerfect 5.1
Advanced WordPerfect 6
Microsoft Word for Windows
Microsoft Word (version 2)
WordStar
Aldus Pagemaker
Microsoft Excel
Lotus 1–2–3
Lotus 1–2–3 for Windows
Lotus 1–2–3 (version 3.4)
SuperCalc
dBase III+
dBase IV (version 2)
Paradox
Microsoft Works
Windows

Typeset by The New Leaf Book Company, Cheltenham, Glos.
Printed and bound in Great Britain at Redwood Books, Trowbridge, Wiltshire.

CONTENTS

USING THIS TUTORIAL

This learning pack is separated into a number of *lessons*. Each lesson covers a specific area and is further split into many graded *examples,* some of which build directly on previous examples. If possible, work through a whole lesson in a single session.

Each lesson ends with a short *test,* enabling you to check that you understand the contents of that lesson. If you are already familiar with some aspects of Works, you could use these tests as a method of revision without going through the complete lesson. Each test is followed by additional exercises to give you extra practice if required.

The lessons build on each other, with each incorporating skills from earlier lessons. However, every lesson is a complete unit, allowing you to pick out only those you require without going through the entire package. This tutorial concentrates on the three main Works applications: word processing, spreadsheets and databases. You can consider these components in any order. You should allow approximately one hour for each lesson. The test and further exercises will take extra time. The actual time will depend largely on your previous experience and keyboard skills.

Following the lessons, at the back of the book, there are some additional exercises covering the main aspects of the work covered in the lessons.

These are followed by an explanation of further Works facilities, some notes on spreadsheets and databases generally, and an introduction to using the mouse.

For quick reference, a summary of procedures is given at the back of the book, together with a section called 'Getting out of Difficulties' in case you have any problems while getting used to working with Microsoft Works.

THE KEYBOARD

If you are not familiar with a computer keyboard, it is worth reading through this introduction before proceeding to the tutorials.

There are a few important keys you should know about:

THE ALT KEY

This is labelled [Alt]. It is used in Works in conjunction with other keys. Pressing **<Alt>** will usually highlight a menu, and you can then choose a required option. The key acts as an alternative to the Mouse.

THE ARROW KEYS

These are labelled [←] [→] [↑] [↓]. On some keyboards they may be included on the extra numeric keypad to the right of the main keyboard.

They are used for moving the cursor around the screen: left, right, up or down and can be used when selecting options on a menu.

THE BACKSPACE KEY

This is labelled [←] and is situated at the top right-hand corner of the letters keyboard. It can be used to delete characters already typed in. Press this once and you will delete the preceding character.

THE CAPS LOCK KEY

This is labelled [Caps Lock]. Its position varies from keyboard to keyboard. If you press this once, the Caps Lock light will come on and any letters you type will be produced in capitals. Pressing **<Caps Lock>** again will turn it off.

THE ESCAPE KEY

This is usually labelled [Esc]. It can be a very useful key! In Works, pressing the Escape key (**<Esc>**) will cancel what you are doing at that moment and takes you back a stage. Generally, pressing **<Esc>** takes you out of the menus and back into the file you are currently using.

THE RETURN KEY

This often looks like [↵] and is a large key situated to the right of the letter keys. It may be labelled Enter or Return instead of being marked with an arrow.

The Return or Enter key is used to enter information. It can be used wherever you are asked to press **<Return>** in the tutorial.

THE SHIFT KEY

This often looks like [⇧]. There are two shift keys on your keyboard situated to the left and right of the letters.

The key is used for two reasons:
i)   It produces capital letters.
        Hold **<Shift>** down and press a letter and you will obtain a capital letter.

ii) It produces alternative characters.
Some keys have two characters printed on them. For example, near the top right-hand corner of the main keyboard you will see the key $\boxed{\pm}$. If you press this, it produces '='
If you hold the **<Shift>** key down and also press this key, you get: +

Try this yourself with other keys. For example, type ? or * using the Shift key.

GETTING STARTED

WHAT IS MICROSOFT WORKS?

Microsoft Works is a very useful integrated package. It contains a number of tools including:

- word processor
- spreadsheet and charting
- database
- communications
- accessories.

This learning pack considers the use of the word processing, spreadsheet, charting and database facilities. A lesson is also included to show how these tools are integrated.

You will need a disk that has already been formatted. Later on, you will be required to create documents and save them on your disk, so it is important that you have a disk ready.

LOADING WORKS

The following instructions assume that Works has been copied onto your hard disk. If you are using it from a floppy disk, refer to the Works manual to see how to set up this package.

1   The operating system should be loaded and the system prompt **C>** displayed.

   If Works has been copied onto your hard disk, it is probably stored in a sub-directory (e.g. C:\WORKS).

2   Type **CD\WORKS <Return>**
   (to change to the correct sub-directory).

3   Load the Works package as follows:

   Type **WORKS <Return>** at the system prompt.

   You will see the following screen:

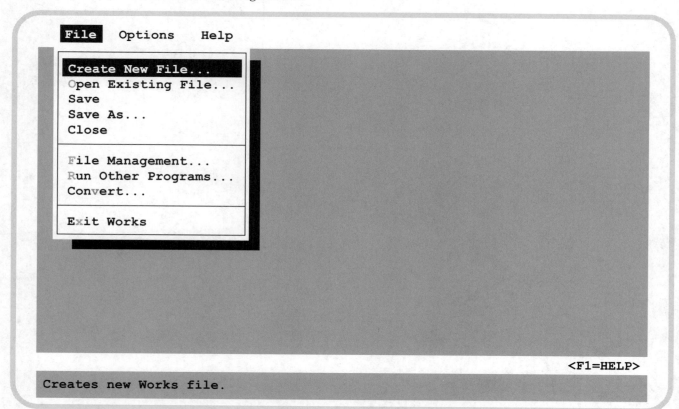

Options can be chosen in one of three ways:

i)   by moving the highlighted cursor with the arrow keys and pressing **<Return>**, *or*
ii) by pressing the initial letter of the option required, *or*
iii) by using the mouse to move the arrow onto the required option and then clicking the mouse button.

The following exercise will help to make you familiar with choosing options within Works. (If you are already familiar with using other menu-driven packages you may wish to proceed directly to the lessons.)

CHOOSING OPTIONS

1 Following the program loading, three options will appear at the top of your screen. They are **File** **Options** and **Help**

Choose **Options**

You can do this by any *one* of the following:

i)   use the arrow keys to move the highlight onto **Options** or
ii) press the **<Alt>** key and type **O** or
iii) use the mouse to move the arrow onto **Options** and click the button.

2 Now, having chosen **Options** the following sub-menu appears as shown below:

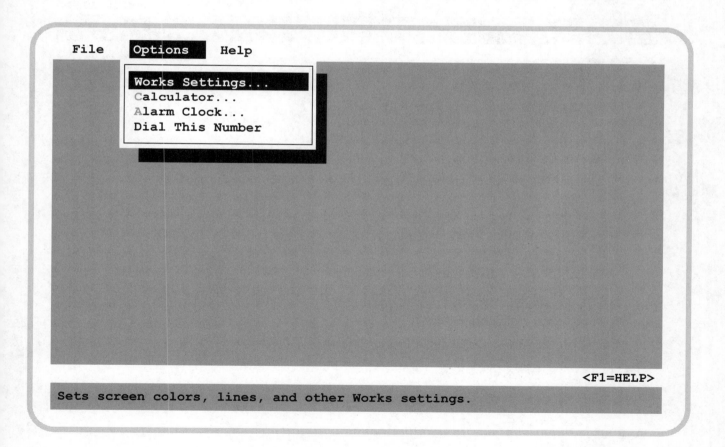

3 Now choose the **Calculator** option.

Either:
i)   Move the highlight to **Calculator** and press **<Return>** or
ii) type **C** or
iii) click the mouse on the **Calculator** option.

The following screen will be displayed:

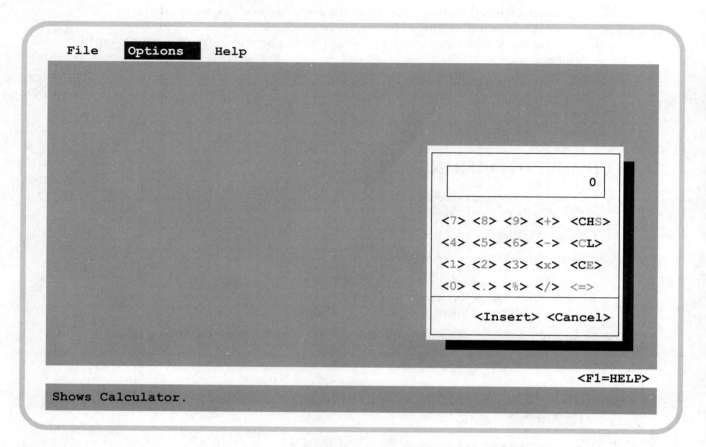

4 You now have your own personal calculator!

Type **3 + 4 =**

The result will be displayed in the calculator.

Alternatively, you can use the mouse and click on the appropriate calculator 'keys'.

For example, click on **<5>**
click on **<+>**
click on **<7>**
click on **<=>**

The result is now displayed on the calculator.

5 Press **<Esc>** to clear the screen and return to the Works main menu.

6 Press **<Alt>** to highlight the menu.

You are now ready to start using Microsoft Works.

Lesson 1

INTRODUCTION TO WORD PROCESSING

In this session we will look at the basic word processing facilities available within Works.

At the end of this lesson you will be able to:

- create a document
- save a document
- insert and delete text
- highlight text
- print a document.

Load Works. The Works Main Menu will be displayed on your screen.

EXAMPLE 1: LOADING THE WORD PROCESSING PACKAGE

Load the word processing package and display a blank screen.

METHOD

1 Choose **File** and **Create New File**

NOTES

Options can be chosen in any one of three ways:
i)   using the mouse, move the arrow to the required option and click the button
ii) using the arrow keys, move the highlight to the required option and press **<Return>**
iii) type the highlighted letter of the required option, (e.g. N for Create New File).

The screen will be displayed as shown at the top of the next page.

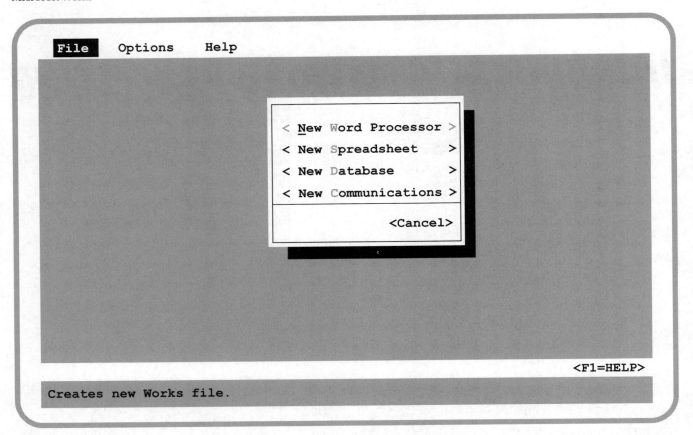

2 Choose   **New Word Processor**

(either click on this option or type **W**).

A blank screen will now be displayed:

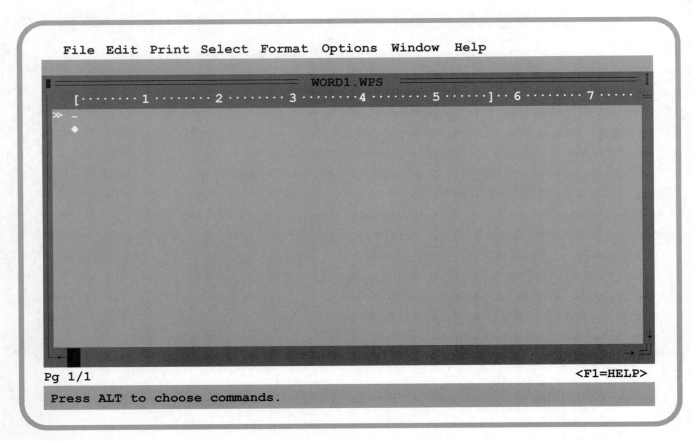

EXAMPLE 2: CREATING A DOCUMENT

Produce a document containing a short piece of text.

Use the text given below for your document:

> The WORKS package consists of a range of software tools including Word Processor, Spreadsheet and Database. Lesson 1 will give you an introduction to the word processing facilities in WORKS.

Ensure a blank screen is displayed before you start.

METHOD

1 Type in the text as given above.

NOTES

You do not need to press **<Return>** at the end of each line. The word processor will automatically do this when a line is filled up.

If you make a mistake, the **<Backspace>** key can be used to delete preceding characters.

To obtain capitals, hold the **<Shift>** key down when typing a letter.

The screen will now contain the required text as shown below.

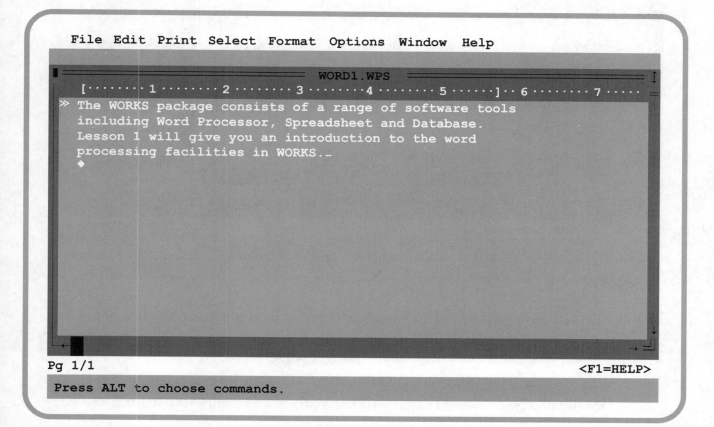

```
 File  Edit  Print  Select  Format  Options  Window  Help

                                WORD1.WPS
    [········1·······2·······3·······4·······5·····]··6·······7·····
 » The WORKS package consists of a range of software tools
   including Word Processor, Spreadsheet and Database.
   Lesson 1 will give you an introduction to the word
   processing facilities in WORKS._
   ◆




Pg 1/1                                                      <F1=HELP>
 Press ALT to choose commands.
```

EXAMPLE 3: SAVING A DOCUMENT

Save the document you produced in Example 2 as a file called INTRO.

METHOD

1 Choose **File**

(click on the **File** option or press **\<Alt>** and then **F**).

2 Choose **Save**

(click on the **Save** option or press **S**).

The following screen is displayed.

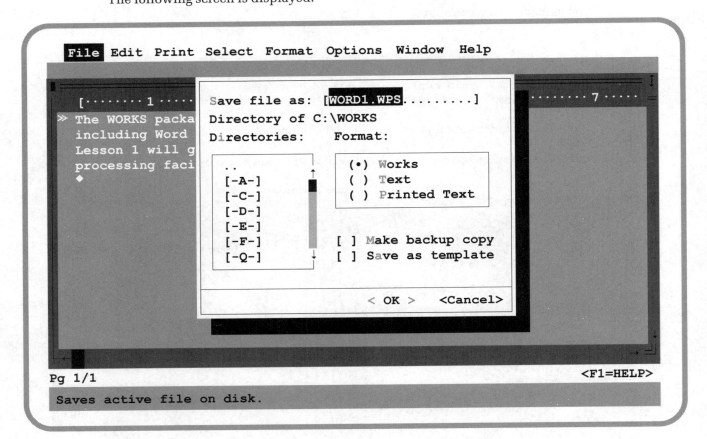

3 On this screen you choose the filename for your document and specify the drive/directory where you require it to be saved.

The filename is currently displayed as **WORD1.WPS**

Type in the required filename: **INTRO**

Note the current directory (e.g. C:\WORKS). Your document will be saved in this directory.

4 Press **\<Return>** or click on **\<OK>** to save the file.

The document has now been saved as a file called INTRO.WPS on the current directory (e.g. C:\WORKS).

(All word-processed documents will have .WPS following the filename when you save them.)

EXAMPLE 4: SAVING IN A DIFFERENT DIRECTORY

Save the current file as INTRO on Drive A.

Ensure that you have a formatted disk in Drive A of your computer.

METHOD

1 Choose File

(Press **<Alt>** and then **F** or click on File).

2 Choose Save As

(Type **A** or click on the Save As option).

3 Type **A:INTRO <Return>**

You have now saved a file called INTRO.WPS onto Drive A.

EXAMPLE 5: CLEARING THE SCREEN

Erase the current document from your screen.

METHOD

1 Choose File

(Press **<Alt>** and then **F** or click on the File option).

2 Choose Close

(Type **C** or click on the Close option).

If you have made any changes to the document since saving it, you will be asked whether you wish to save again. Choose Yes or No

The screen is now cleared and the Works Main Menu is displayed.

EXAMPLE 6: LOADING AND EDITING A FILE

Load the INTRO file from Drive A and make the following changes to a document:

i)   Insert a title: 'INTRODUCTION TO WORKS'.
ii)   Insert 'Communications,' after 'Word Processor,' in the first sentence.
iii) In the second sentence, delete 'Lesson 1' and replace it with 'This lesson'.

METHOD

1 Choose File and Open Existing File

2 Type **A:INTRO <Return>**

This document will now be displayed on your screen.

3 Use the arrow keys to move the cursor to the beginning of the text.

4 Type **INTRODUCTION TO WORKS**

Notice that all existing text is moved along to make room for this title.

5 Now press **<Return>**

The text at the cursor is moved to a new line.

6 Press **<Return>** again.

We now have a blank line between the title and text.

7 Move the cursor to the space between 'Word Processor,' and 'Spreadsheet' in the first sentence and type **Communications,**

8 Move the cursor to the beginning of the second sentence in order to delete 'Lesson 1'.

Press the **<Delete>** key. One character is deleted.

Keep pressing **<Delete>** until the required text has been deleted.

Notice that the remaining text is moved inwards to replace the deleted text.

9 Now type **This lesson**

The screen will now look like the one at the top of the next page.

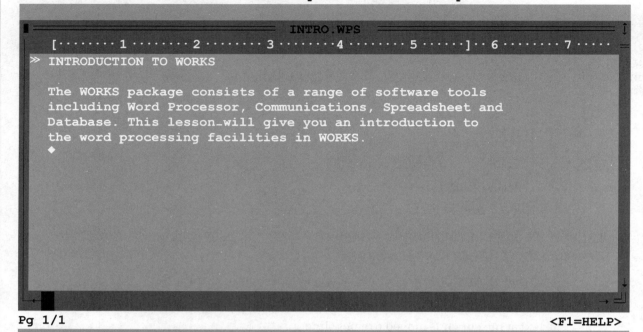

```
    File  Edit  Print  Select  Format  Options  Window  Help
┌─────────────────────────────────────────────────────────────────────┐
│                            INTRO.WPS                                  │↑
│  [········1········2········3········4········5·····]··6········7····· │
│>> INTRODUCTION TO WORKS                                               │
│                                                                       │
│   The WORKS package consists of a range of software tools            │
│   including Word Processor, Communications, Spreadsheet and          │
│   Database. This lesson will give you an introduction to             │
│   the word processing facilities in WORKS.                           │
│   ◆                                                                    │
│                                                                       │
│                                                                       │
│                                                                       │
│                                                                       │
│                                                                       │↓
│                                                                       │
Pg 1/1                                                        <F1=HELP>
Press ALT to choose commands.
```

10 Save this as a file called INTRO2 on Drive A.

Choose **File**

(Press **<Alt>** and then **F** or click on **File**).

Choose **Save As**

Type **A:INTRO2 <Return>**

(Do *not* put spaces in a filename; e.g. INTRO 2 is not an acceptable filename.)

This amended document has now been saved.

EXAMPLE 7: HIGHLIGHTING TEXT

Create a new document containing the following text and include bold and underlining where indicated.

<u>WORD PROCESSING</u>

Word processing enables us to create, edit and print documents quickly and simply. There are many such word processing packages on the market. Other packages, such as **WORKS,** are called 'integrated packages' and include word processing as one of many facilities offered.

Simple word processing packages would allow us to insert or delete text, highlight text by **emboldening** or <u>underlining</u> and include many other features.

METHOD

1 Clear the screen by proceeding as follows:

Choose **File**

Choose **Close**

The screen is now cleared.

2 We are now going to create a new word processing file:

Choose **Create New File**

Choose **New Word Processor**

A blank screen is now shown.

3 We wish to underline the title line in this document:

Choose **Format** (press **<Alt>** and **T** or click on **Format**).

The screen display now looks like this:

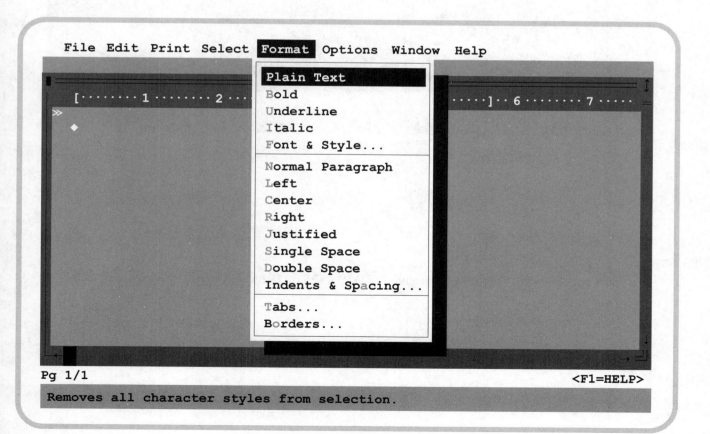

4 Choose **Underline**

Type **WORD PROCESSING**

You will see that this text is automatically underlined as you type.

5 Now to turn the underlining off:

Choose **Format**

Choose **Plain Text**

6 Continue to type the text using bold and underline when required.

If you wish to embolden any text, turn it on by using **Format** and **Bold**

When you wish to return to ordinary text, choose **Format** and **Plain Text**

7 Complete the text as given at the beginning of this example.

The following document will be displayed:

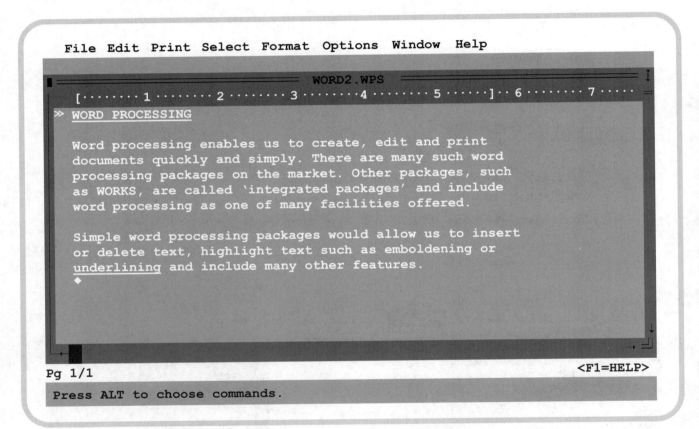

8 Save this document:

Choose **File**

Choose **Save As**

Type **A:WP1 <Return>**

The document has now been saved as WP1.WPS on Drive A.

EXAMPLE 8: PRINTING A DOCUMENT

Print out the document previously created.

The WP1 document should still be displayed on the screen.

METHOD

1 Choose **Print**

(Press **<Alt>** then **P** or click on the **Print** option).

2 Choose **Print** again.

The 'Number of copies' should be set to **1**

3 Press **<Return>**

The document will now be printed out. (If you have problems with this, check that your printer has been set up correctly.)

EXAMPLE 9: EXITING FROM WORKS

Finish using the word processor and exit from Works.

METHOD

1 Choose File

2 Choose Exit Works

If you have made any changes to the current document since the last time you saved it, you will be asked whether you wish to save again.

Choose Yes if you wish to resave or No if you wish to exit without saving.

You have been taken out of Works and the system prompt (e.g. C:\WORKS) is now displayed.

TEST

1 Load the word processing package and display a blank screen.

2 Create a document with the following text:

Word processing is using a computer to create letters, memos, charts or any other document that you can create on a typewriter.

You first write or create the documents and save them on a diskette or hard disk. Whatever you type is displayed on the screen. With a word processor, you can easily add to, change, correct or erase single letters, words, paragraphs or entire documents. The document can then be printed as many times as you require.

3 Insert the title 'WHAT IS WORD PROCESSING?' at the top of this document.

4 Delete the sentence 'Whatever you type is displayed on the screen'.

5 Insert a new paragraph at the bottom of the document:

Completed documents are stored electronically on a diskette or hard disk, and can be changed, edited or updated whenever you wish.

6 Save this document as WORD2 on Drive A and exit from Works.

FURTHER EXERCISES

1 i) Create a document containing the following letter:

Dear Sir

Thank you for your letter dated 25 August requesting a copy of the WORKS package. Details on prices and how to order are enclosed with this letter.

Yours sincerely

William Price

ii) Save this document as ORDER1.
iii) Insert a date and your address at the top of the letter.
iv) Replace 'sincerely' with 'faithfully'.
v) Resave this letter as ORDER1.

2 i) Create a document containing the following text:

Using the WORKS package is easy. If available, it is preferable to use the mouse for most operations. The mouse can be used to choose options displayed on the screen as well as for moving the cursor around the screen.

An alternative to the mouse is to use the standard keyboard. The Alt key can be used to highlight the menus, and arrow keys used to move the cursor around the screen.

ii) Save this document as MOUSE.
iii) Insert and underline the heading: USING THE MOUSE IN WORKS
iv) Insert the word 'relatively' before 'easy' in the first sentence.
v) Delete 'on the screen' in the third sentence.
vi) Resave the document as MOUSE2.

Now proceed to Lesson 2: Further Word Processing.

Lesson 2

FURTHER WORD PROCESSING

In this session we will look at some additional facilities available in the word processing option in Works.

At the end of this lesson you will be able to:

- use tabs
- centre text
- preview a document before printing
- move blocks of text
- search and replace text.

Load Works. The Works Main Menu will be displayed on your screen.

EXAMPLE 1: USING TABS

Produce a document containing the text given below.

	1991	1992	1993	1994
QUARTERLY SALES 1991– 4				
1st Quarter	300	625	720	870
2nd Quarter	450	850	825	885
3rd Quarter	500	700	910	910
4th Quarter	520	600	890	960

The screen should be clear before you start this example.

METHOD

1 Choose **File** and **Create New File**
   Choose **New Word Processor**

2 Type in the heading **QUARTERLY SALES 1991– 94**
   Press **<Return>** twice to move the cursor to a new line.

3 Use the **<Tab>** key to position the years:
   Use the **<Tab>** three times.

   Type **1991**

   Press **<Tab>** twice.
   Type **1992**

   Press **<Tab>** twice.
   Type **1993**

   Press **<Tab>** twice.
   Type **1994**

   Press **<Return>** twice.

4 Type **1st Quarter**

Press **<Tab>**
Type **300**

Press **<Tab>** twice.
Type **625**

Press **<Tab>** twice.
Type **720**

Press **<Tab>** twice.
Type **870**
Press **<Return>**

5 Continue to enter the remaining text in this table, using the Tab key when necessary.

The screen will then look like this:

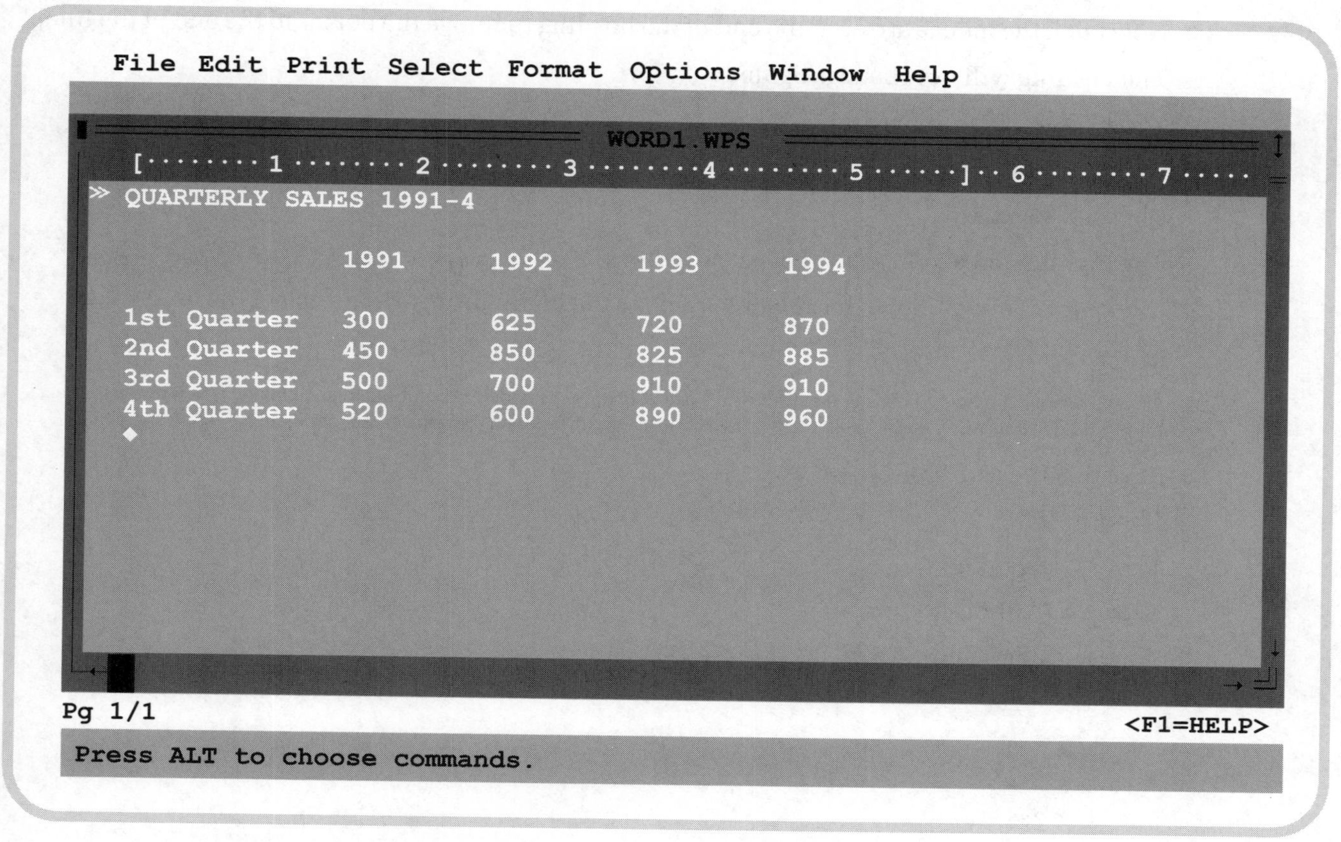

```
 File   Edit   Print   Select   Format   Options   Window   Help

━━━━━━━━━━━━━━━━━━━━━━━━ WORD1.WPS ━━━━━━━━━━━━━━━━━━━━━━━
 [·······1········2·······3········4·······5······]··6········7·····
» QUARTERLY SALES 1991-4


                    1991       1992       1993       1994

 1st Quarter        300        625        720        870
 2nd Quarter        450        850        825        885
 3rd Quarter        500        700        910        910
 4th Quarter        520        600        890        960
 ◆




 Pg 1/1                                                      <F1=HELP>
 Press ALT to choose commands.
```

(The exact layout of your screen may differ from this depending on how the tabs have been set up. Try to produce a document as closely as possible to the example shown above.)

EXAMPLE 2: CENTERING TEXT

Centre the heading of the quarterly sales table produced in Example 1.

METHOD

1 To centre a block of text you must first select it:

Move the cursor to the beginning of the heading.

Choose **Select**

Choose **Text**

2 Now click the mouse arrow at the end of the heading (or move the cursor to the end of the line).

The heading will now be highlighted.

3 To centre the highlighted text:

Choose **Format**

Choose **Centre**

The highlighted text has now been centred.

4 Click the mouse or move the cursor to remove the highlighting (i.e. de-select the text).

NOTES

This method can be used to change the display of existing text; i.e. to underline, embolden and change font type. First select the required text using **Select** and **Text** then choose **Format** with the appropriate option (e.g. **Underline** etc.).

5 Save this file as TABLE in Drive A:

Choose **File**

Choose **Save As**

Type **A:TABLE <Return>**

6 Choose **File** and **Close** to clear the screen.

EXAMPLE 3: PREVIEWING A DOCUMENT

Preview the TABLE document before printing it out.

We wish to preview the document so that we can see how it will be displayed when printed.

METHOD

1 Load the TABLE document:

Choose **File** and **Open Existing File**

Type **A:TABLE <Return>**

The document has now been loaded and displayed on your screen.

2 To preview this document:

Choose **Print**

Choose **Preview**

The screen will now be displayed as shown below:

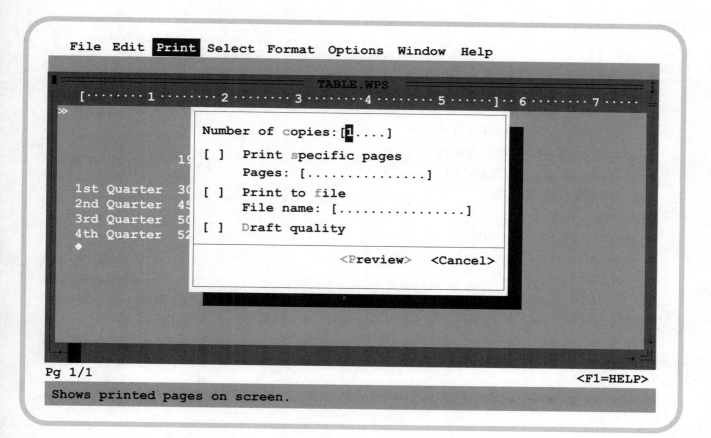

3 This screen shows some print specifications.

Select **Preview**

Either i) Click on **<Preview>**

Or ii) Move the cursor to **<Preview>** and press **<Return>**

The first page in your document is now displayed, showing exactly how it will be printed, as shown at the top of the next page.

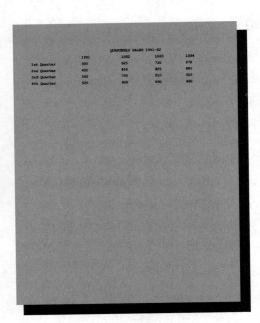

```
Page 1
  QUARTERLY SALES 1991-4...

Press PgUp or PgDn for
  previous or next page.
Press P to print.
Print ESC to cancel.
```

4 Press **P** to print out the document.

The file (TABLE) will now be printed out and you will be returned to the original screen.

5 Clear the screen using the following method:

Choose **File** and **Close**

The Main Menu will now be displayed.

EXAMPLE 4: MOVING BLOCKS OF TEXT

Produce the letter given below. Then edit this letter so that the sentence 'Your letter contained...' is placed immediately after the first sentence 'Thank you for...'.

123 The High Street
Easthampton
PX21 4KB

1 June 1992

Dear Mrs Smith

Thank you for your letter dated 25 May. We have an extensive range of the items you require and I enclose a brochure together with the latest price list. Your letter contained a detailed list of requirements. The following items are always in stock:

Print Ribbons
Diskettes
Stationery.

If you require any further details, please do not hesitate to contact me.

Yours sincerely

B Morris

Marketing Manager

METHOD

1 Choose **File** and **Create New File**

Choose **New Word Processor**

A blank document is now displayed.

2 Type in the letter as given above, using tabs when required.

3 To move text we must first select it:

Move the cursor to the beginning of the sentence 'Your letter contained...'

Choose **Select**

Choose **Text**

Now move the cursor to the end of the required sentence.

(Use the arrow keys to move the cursor, or click the mouse on the end of the sentence.)

The sentence has now been highlighted.

4 Choose **Edit**

Choose **Move**

5 Move the cursor to the new position for the beginning of the sentence.

Press **<Return>**

The text will now be placed in the new position.

(Using the same method, a whole block of text can be copied or deleted. Select the text first, then use Edit.)

6 Save this document as LETTER 1 on Drive A.

EXAMPLE 5: SEARCHING AND REPLACING TEXT

Using the LETTER1 document, replace all the occurrences of 'list' with the word 'specification'.

The LETTER1 document should be displayed on the screen.

METHOD

1 Move the cursor to the beginning of the document.

2 Choose **Select**

Choose **Replace**

3 **Search for**

Type **list** (Do *not* press **<Return>**)

4 Move the cursor to the next line.

Replace with:

Type **specification** (Do *not* press **<Return>**)

5 Choose **Replace All**

You are informed how many occurrences have been replaced.

6 Choose **OK**

Look at your letter to see where the replacements have occurred.

7 Try the Search and Replace technique again by replacing the original words (i.e. replace 'specification' with 'list').

8 Clear the screen.

TEST

1 Create a new document called SEC as shown below:

THE SECRETARY

A competent secretary is indispensable and could even be considered to be priceless. But clearly the secretary of today is more expensive than the secretary of a few years ago. Today top secretaries are in fairly short supply; partly because firms are demanding higher and higher qualifications, but also because they now demand a wide knowledge of the latest technology available to firms.

Many employers claim that their secretaries are not as responsible as they should be, and do not take the trouble to learn enough about the business. Some even suggest that their secretaries do not apply enough business sense or work conscientiously. Others consider that standards have fallen both in the ability to communicate with others and in the standards of typewriting, etc. Most employers, however, would agree that standards have been raised and that the secretarial job today demands more basic intelligence, more formal education, more initiative and smarter dressing; in that order.

Other qualities which are sought are an ability to manage, human relations skills and punctuality; while loyalty and devotion both to the job and the organisation are taken for granted. How does the employer hold on to a reliable secretary? Most employers would agree that financial rewards may be the final and crucial factor.

2 Move the sentence 'Most employers, however,...' to a position above the second paragraph. Make this a new paragraph on its own and delete 'however,'.

3 Copy the sentence (in the final paragraph) 'How does the employer...' to the beginning of the final paragraph. This sentence should now appear twice, so delete the second occurrence.

4 Centre the heading.

5 Preview this document before printing.

6 Save this document as SEC.

FURTHER EXERCISES

1 i) Erase the screen (ensure that you have already saved the previous document).
   ii) Create a new document containing the following details:

Employee	Grade	Salary
A SMITH	A12	£14,500
E HEATH	B13	£18,175
B JONES	B17	£12,500
F HARVEY	CO2	£9,200
C BROWN	AO6	£16,750
D BROOKES	A04	£21,200
E THOMAS	B14	£12,140
L NEVILLE	A07	£19,150
M GREGORY	C11	£16,250
H WRIGHT	B19	£13,120

   Use the tab key to create this table.
   iii) Insert a title for this table: EMPLOYEE SUMMARY
   iv) Underline the title.
   v) Move the HARVEY, BROWN and BROOKES details to the end of the list.
   vi) Preview this document before printing.
   vii) Save this document as EMPLOYEE and erase the screen.

2 i) Create a table of names and addresses as shown below.

J Brand 2 New Hill Glasgow	R Rubens 34 The Walkway Coventry
S Singh 269 High Street Plymouth	E Gregory 49 Wilton Avenue Ramsgate
A Forsyth 177 Jarvis Close Newquay	B Jung 85 The Avenue Londonderry

   ii) Insert a title: MAILING LIST
   iii) Change the address of A Forsyth to 243 Winter Close, Barnstaple.
   iv) Embolden each name in this list (not the address).
   v) Save the file as MAILING.
   vi) With the cursor at the top of the document, search for 'E Gregory' and replace with 'E Thomas'.
   vii) Resave the file as MAILING.

Now proceed to Lesson 3: Introduction to Spreadsheets.

Lesson 3

INTRODUCTION TO SPREADSHEETS

In this session we will look at the basic spreadsheet facilities available in Works. If you have not previously used spreadsheets you should refer to the section headed 'Notes on Spreadsheets' on page 89 before proceeding with this lesson.

At the end of this lesson you will be able to:

- create spreadsheets
- save and retrieve spreadsheets
- move from cell to cell
- use formulae
- print spreadsheets.

Load Works. The Works Menu will be displayed on your screen.

EXAMPLE 1: LOADING THE SPREADSHEET PACKAGE

Load the Spreadsheet package and display a blank spreadsheet.

METHOD

1 Choose `File` and `Create New File`

NOTES

Options can be chosen in any one of three ways:
  i) using the mouse, move the arrow to the required option and click the button; *or*
  ii) using the arrow keys, move the highlight to the required option and press `<Return>` ; *or*
  iii) type the highlighted letter of the required option: e.g. **N** for Create New File.

The screen will now look like the one at the top of the next page.

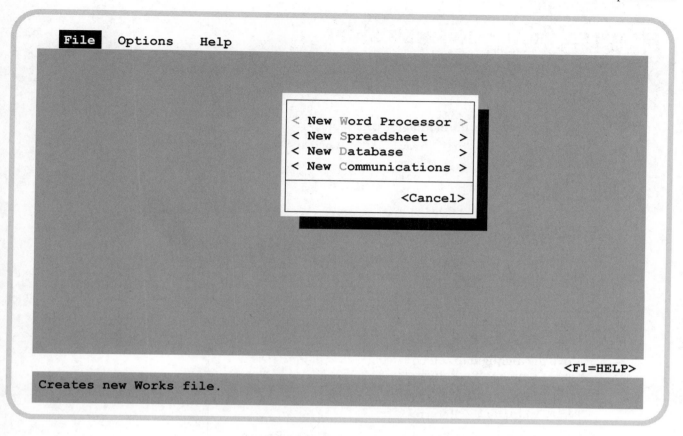

2 Choose **New Spreadsheet**

(Either click on this option or type **S**)

A blank (new) spreadsheet will be displayed as shown below:

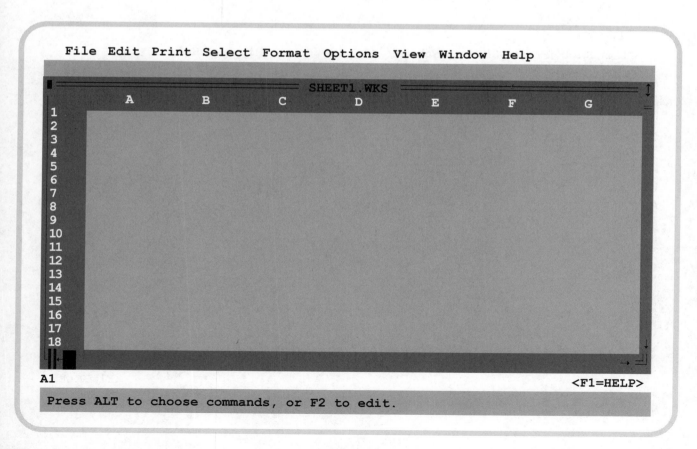

EXAMPLE 2: CREATING A SPREADSHEET

Create a table showing the sales figures for two companies over a three-year period.

Use the following information for your table:

Year	Company X	Company Y
1990	300	420
1991	390	440
1992	450	380

METHOD

1 A highlight is shown in cell A1. This can be moved around the screen by using the arrow keys or clicking the mouse where required. Try this now.

2 Insert the table:

Move the highlight to cell A1.
Type **Year** **<Return>**

Move the highlight to cell C1.
Type **Company X** **<Return>**

Move the highlight to cell E1.
Type **Company Y** **<Return>**

3 Now move the highlight to cell A3. Type **1990** **<Return>**

Move the highlight to cell C3. Type **300** **<Return>**

Move the highlight to cell E3. Type **420** **<Return>**

4 Continue entering the data for the remaining two years.

The table will be displayed as shown below:

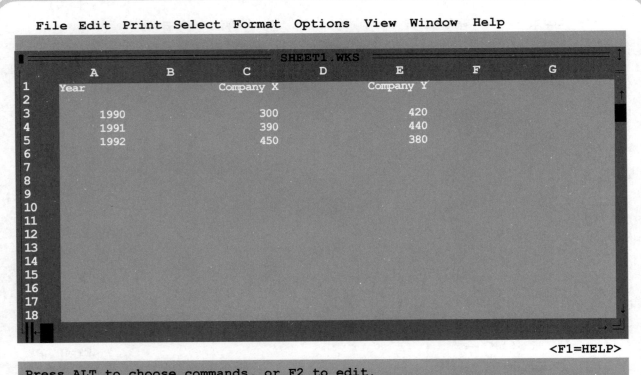

EXAMPLE 3: SAVING A SPREADSHEET

Save the current table as a file called SALES.

The spreadsheet should be displayed on your screen as created in Example 2. Ensure that you have a disk in Drive A.

METHOD

1 Choose **File**

(Click on **File** or press **<Alt>** and then **F**)

The following screen is displayed:

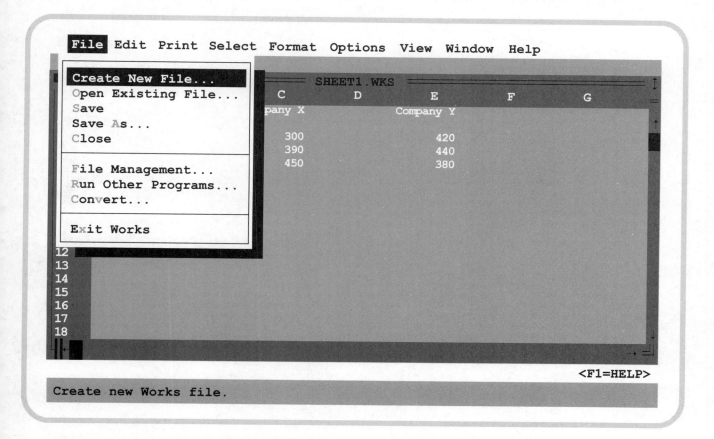

2 Choose **Save As**

(Click on **Save As** or type **A**)

3 Type **A:SALES** **<Return>**

The spreadsheet has now been saved on Drive A as a file called SALES.WKS. (All spreadsheets will have .WKS following the filename when you save them.)

EXAMPLE 4: CLEARING THE SCREEN

Erase the current spreadsheet.

METHOD

1 Choose **File**

(Press **<Alt>** and then **F** or click on **File**).

Choose **Close**

(Type **C** or click on the **Close** option).

2 If you have made any changes to the spreadsheet since last saving it, you will be asked whether you wish to save these changes. Just choose **Yes** or **No**

The spreadsheet will now be cleared and the Works Main Menu will be displayed.

EXAMPLE 5: LOADING A SPREADSHEET

Load the file SALES onto the screen and insert details on a third company (Company Z) with sales of 650, 510 and 490 over the same three-year period.

METHOD

1 Choose **File** and **Open Existing File**

Type **A:SALES <Return>**

NOTES

If you have problems loading this file, type **A:SALES.WKS<Return>**
The extension **.WKS** is used for all spreadsheet files.

The spreadsheet will now be displayed.

2 Move the highlight to cell G1.
Type **Company Z**

3 Move the highlight to type the three sales figures for this company in cells G3, G4 and G5.

4 Save this file as SALES2:

Choose **File**

Choose **Save As**

Type **A:SALES2 <Return>** (Do *not* put spaces in a filename; e.g. SALES 2 is not acceptable as a filename.)

This amended spreadsheet has now been saved.

EXAMPLE 6: USING FORMULAE

Insert formulae into the table used in Example 5 to calculate the total sales figures for each company over the three-year period.

The SALES2 spreadsheet should be displayed on your screen.

METHOD

1 Move the highlight to cell A7.
  Type **Total Sales** **<Return>**

2 Move the highlight to cell C7.
  Type **= C3 + C4 + C5** **<Return>**

  The result of adding the three cells (C3, C4 and C5) is displayed in this cell.

  (*Note:* Always type = before entering a formula into a cell.)

3 Move the highlight to cell E7.
  Type **= E3 + E4 + E5** **<Return>**

4 Move the highlight to cell G7.
  Type **= G3 + G4 + G5** **<Return>**

  The formulae have now all been inserted and the resulting spreadsheet will look like this:

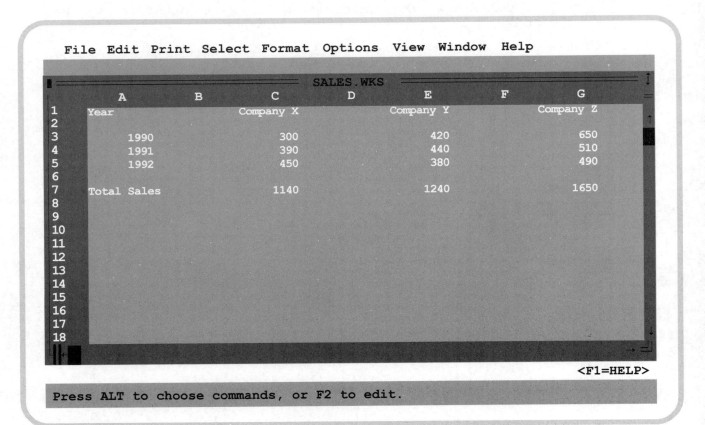

5 Now save this spreadsheet using the same name (SALES2).

  Choose **File** and **Save**

  The file will now be saved on Drive A as SALES2.WKS.

  (Note that the Save option can be used when saving a file under the same name in the same drive.)

EXAMPLE 7: PRINTING A SPREADSHEET

Print out the SALES2 spreadsheet.

The SALES2 spreadsheet containing sales figures for three companies should be displayed.

METHOD

1 Choose Print

(Click on Print or press **<Alt>** and then **P**).

2 Choose Print again

(Click on **<Print>** or press **P**).

Some print specifications are now displayed including the number of copies required.

3 Choose Print

(Click on Print or use the arrow keys to move the cursor down to this option and press **<Return>**)

A print-out of the spreadsheet will now be obtained. (If you have problems with printing, ensure that the printer is connected and has been set up correctly.)

NOTES

If a spreadsheet does not fit onto a single page you may find a number of pages are printed. Each page will contain a number of columns from the spreadsheet. In this example, you may obtain a print-out of this table on two pages.

4 Finally, clear the screen by choosing **File** and **Close**

The screen is now cleared and the Main Menu displayed.

TEST

1 Create a spreadsheet containing the following information on monthly costs.

	January	February	March
Mortgage	600	600	580
Services	140	160	170
Food	270	240	280
Travel	95	90	100
Insurance	25	32	26

2 Save this spreadsheet as COSTS and erase the screen.

3 Load the COSTS spreadsheet again and insert a row containing formulae for the total costs in each month shown.

4 Insert an extra column for April entering values for the costs in this month, and calculate the total costs.

5 Save this spreadsheet as COSTS2 and obtain a print-out.

FURTHER EXERCISES

1 i) Create a spreadsheet containing details on attendances at training courses.

	Course 1	Course 2
Monday	42	30
Tuesday	40	31
Wednesday	38	28
Thursday	34	29
Friday	36	29

ii) Save this spreadsheet as COURSE.
iii) Insert formulae to calculate the total numbers attending each course and the totals on each day.
iv) Resave the spreadsheet and obtain a print-out.

2 i) Create a spreadsheet containing the income and costs for a company over four quarters in 1993.

	1st Qtr	2nd Qtr	3rd Qtr	4th Qtr
Income	23,000	25,000	32,000	27,000
Costs	19,000	21,500	20,400	22,300

ii) Insert an extra row to calculate the profit in each quarter for this company.
(Profit = Income - Costs.)
iii) Insert formulae to calculate totals for the income, costs and profit in 1993.
iv) Now change the costs to 23,000 in each quarter.
iv) Save the spreadsheet as PROFIT and print it out.

This concludes Lesson 3 in the Works course. You are now ready to continue with Lesson 4: Further Spreadsheets.

Lesson 4:

FURTHER SPREADSHEETS

In this session we will consider some additional features available using spreadsheets in Works.

At the end of this lesson you will be able to:

- insert and delete lines
- copy cells and ranges
- format cells
- change column widths
- preview printing.

Load Works. The Works Main Menu will be displayed on your screen.

EXAMPLE 1: INSERTING LINES

Produce a spreadsheet containing the details given below, then insert two new departments.

Department	Gross Profit	Costs
Hardware	70	200
Toys	40	500
Stationery	50	250

The two extra departments to be inserted between 'Hardware' and 'Toys' are as follows:

Fashion	40	320
Catering	16	400

METHOD

1 Choose **File** and **Create New File**

2 Choose **New Spreadsheet**

3 Insert the information given in the table into a spreadsheet as follows:

Move to cell A1.
Type **Department**

Similarly, in cell C1 type **Gross Profit** and in cell E1 type **Costs**

Move to A3 and type **Hardware**
Move to A4 and type **Toys**
Move to A5 and type **Stationery**

Complete the table by inserting data in the appropriate cells.

4 We now wish to insert two extra rows.

Move the highlight to cell A4.

The two rows will be inserted at this part of the spreadsheet:

Choose **Edit**

The screen will now look like the one at the top of the next page.

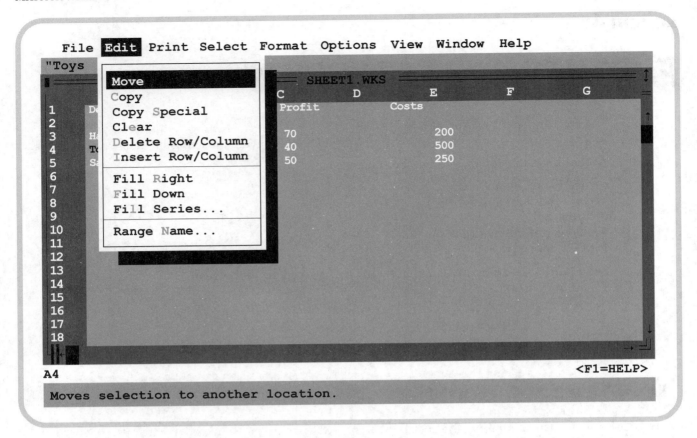

5 Choose **Insert Row/Column**

In the next screen you must choose whether to insert a row or column.

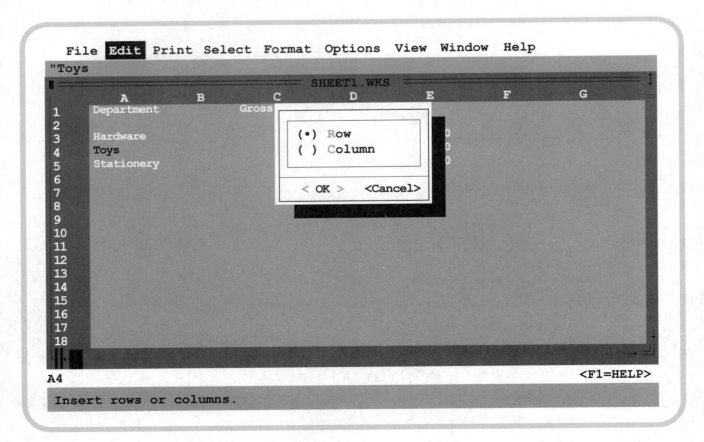

The dot by 'Row' indicates that this is chosen.

6 Choose <OK>

(Either click on <OK> using the mouse or just press <Return>)

A new row appears at the required place in your table.

7 Repeat this process to insert an extra blank row.

8 Now type in the new data.

9 The following spreadsheet will be displayed:

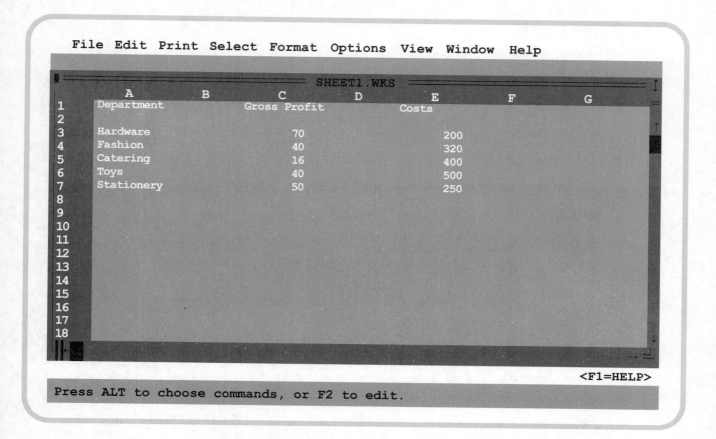

10 To save this spreadsheet as DEPT proceed as follows:

Choose File

Choose Save As

Type **A:DEPT** **<Return>**

The file has now been saved as DEPT.WKS on Drive A.

Microsoft Works

EXAMPLE 2: COPYING CELLS

Experiment with copying one cell or a range of cells to another part of the table.

METHOD

1 For example, try to copy 'Department' to another part of the table.

Move the highlight to the cell containing 'Department', e.g. A1.

2 Choose **Edit**

Choose **Copy**

3 Move the highlight to a new cell, e.g. C14.

Press **<Return>**

You will see that the contents of A1 have been copied into C14.

4 Now try to copy the top line containing all the headings to another part of the table.

Move the highlight to A1.

Select the range of cells you wish to copy, e.g. A1 across to E1.

NOTES

The range of cells can be selected in one of two ways:
i) click the mouse on A1 and, holding the mouse button down, move the pointer to the end of the required range, i.e. E1 *or*
ii) choose **Select** and **Cells** then use the arrow keys to highlight the required range, e.g. A1 to E1.

5 Once the required range has been highlighted:

Choose **Edit**

Choose **Copy**

6 Move the highlight to the start of the new range, e.g. A16.

Press **<Return>**

The range of cells A1 to E1 has been copied to the cells starting at A16.

7 Finally, delete the extra lines in rows 14 and 16 by using **Edit** and **Delete**

In the same way, cells can be moved from one part of a spreadsheet to another. Experiment with this using **Edit** and **Move**

EXAMPLE 3: COPYING TO A RANGE

Insert an extra column in the DEPT file, giving the percentage profit gained in each department.

METHOD

1 To obtain the percentage profit we must divide the Gross Profit by Costs and then multiply by 100.

So, in general, Percentage Profit = Gross Profit / Costs * 100

(The symbol for Division is / and for Multiplication is *)

2 Move to cell G3.
Type **= C3/E3*100 <Return>**
(Remember to put = before typing in the formula.)

The result of the formula (i.e. 35) will appear in cell G3. This tells us that the Hardware Department gets a 35% profit.

3 We could enter a similar formula for each of the other departments. Instead, we will COPY the formula down to the other cells.

4 The highlight is on cell G3.

Select the range G3 down to G7.

(Do this either by clicking the mouse on G3 and, holding the button down, move the arrow down to cell G7; or, choose **Select** and **Cells** and use the arrow keys to highlight the required cells.)

5 With the appropriate range of cells highlighted, proceed as follows:

Choose **Edit**

Choose **Fill Down**

The formula has now been inserted and calculated in all the highlighted cells.

6 Finally, type the heading 'Percentage' for column G and save this spreadsheet as DEPT2.

EXAMPLE 4: FORMATTING CELLS

Change the gross profit and costs values to a Currency format.

Data can be displayed in different ways by using the Format option.

Ensure the DEPT2 table is displayed before starting this example.

METHOD

1 Select the range of cells you wish to format:

i.e. C3 down to E7, which contains the values for Gross Profit and Costs.

2 The required range will now be highlighted.

Choose **Format**

The following spreadsheet will be displayed:

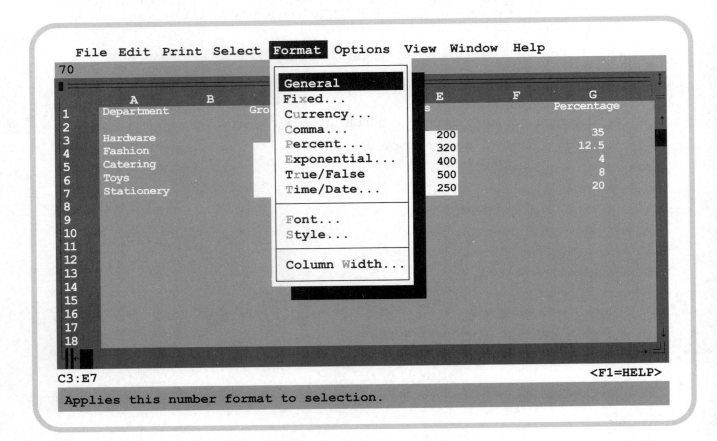

3 Choose **Currency**

Press **<Return>** to display these values with 2 decimal places.

EXAMPLE 5: CHANGING COLUMN WIDTHS

Change the width of Column A to 15, and reduce the width of Columns B to G down to 8.

METHOD

1 Move the highlight to any cell in Column A; e.g. A1.

Choose **Format**

Choose **Column Width**

Type **15 <Return>**

2 The width of Column A has now been increased. You will see that Column G can no longer be displayed on the screen.

3 Now highlight cells B1 to G1.

(Do not worry if you cannot see all the cells at the same time on the screen.)

The highlighted range (B1:G1) will now be displayed at the foot of the screen.

4 Choose **Format**

Choose **Column Width**

Type **8 <Return>**

5 Now move the highlight back to A1.

The widths of columns have now been adjusted as required.

EXAMPLE 6: VIEWING AND PRINTING

Obtain a print-out of the DEPT2 spreadsheet on *one* sheet by reducing the column widths if required.

METHOD

1 We can obtain a view of how the spreadsheet will look when printed without actually printing it out.

Choose **Print**

Choose **Preview**

Press **<Return>** or click on **<Preview>**

2 The screen now displays a view of the first page when printed. Press **<Page Down>** to view the next page.

3 At the moment, not all of the columns can be printed on one page.

Press **<Esc>** to go back to the spreadsheet.

4 Try to reduce the width of the first column to 8 by doing the following:

Move the highlight to A1.

Choose **Format**

Choose **Column Width**

Type **8 <Return>**

The width of Column A has now been reduced.

5 Now preview the spreadsheet before printing:

Choose **Print**

Choose **Preview**

Press **<Return>** or click on **<Preview>**

You will see that the spreadsheet can now be printed on one page.

Press **P** to obtain a print-out.

6 Save this spreadsheet using the same name (DEPT2):

Choose **File**

Choose **Save**

The spreadsheet has been resaved under the same name.

TEST

1 Create a spreadsheet containing the following details on household expenses:

	1991	1992	1993
Rent	2000	2200	2400
Electricity	800	900	1050
Food	3200	3300	3500
Gas	500	560	550

2 Insert an extra row between Rent and Electricity giving the Travel expenses equal to 600, 700 and 790 over the three years.

3 Include a row giving the total expenses in each year 1991–3.

4 Display the values in Currency format with no decimal places.

5 Preview this spreadsheet before printing.

6 Save this table as EXP.

FURTHER EXERCISES

1 i) Create a spreadsheet containing the following information:

PRODUCTION FIGURES

	Dept C	Dept S	Dept D	Dept M
Week 1	300	450	290	310
Week 2	320	420	350	320
Week 3	330	390	310	350
Week 4	320	370	360	370
Week 5	340	340	350	410

ii) Insert a formula to calculate the total production in Dept C over the five-week period. Copy this formula across to obtain the other departmental totals.

iii) Move the Dept M column in between Dept C and Dept S. Ensure that all totals are still calculated.

iv) Preview this table before printing. Adjust column widths if required to print the table on one page.

2 i) Create a spreadsheet containing the following information:

INCOME PROJECTION

	Jan–Mar	Apr–Jun	Jul–Sep	Oct–Dec
SALES INCOME	26,000	54,000	76,500	59,500
SALARIES	5,000	6,000	6,000	6,000
PURCHASES	12,000	15,000	12,500	14,500
RENT AND RATES	4,000	4,000	4,000	4,000

ii) Re-format the spreadsheet so that the first column is 15 characters wide and the remaining columns are 12 characters wide.

iii) Reformat the numbers into Currency with 2 decimal places.

iv) Insert two further rows:

The first new row to give the TOTAL COSTS in each period (i.e. the sum of SALARIES, PURCHASES and RENT AND RATES).

The second additional row to give the PROFIT in each period (i.e. the SALES INCOME minus the TOTAL COSTS).

v) Ensure that the extra rows are displayed in an appropriate format, then print out the spreadsheet.

You are now ready to go on to Lesson 5: Charts.

Lesson 5:

CHARTS

In this session we will deal with the basic graphical facilities available in Works. Graphs are referred to as 'Charts' in the Works package.

At the end of this lesson you will be able to:

- create a graph
- amend graph settings
- incorporate legends and titles
- change graph types
- print out graphs.

Load Works. The Works Main Menu will be displayed on your screen.

EXAMPLE 1: CREATING A SPREADSHEET

Produce a spreadsheet containing the details given below.

COMPANY SALES IN 1993

	1st QTR	2nd QTR	3rd QTR	4th QTR
COMPANY X	600	500	580	680
COMPANY Y	700	670	720	730
COMPANY Z	740	690	680	720

Ensure that the screen is clear before starting this example.

METHOD

1 Choose **File**

   Choose **Create New File**

   Choose **New Spreadsheet**

2 Type in the details given above. Your screen will now look like the one shown on the next page.

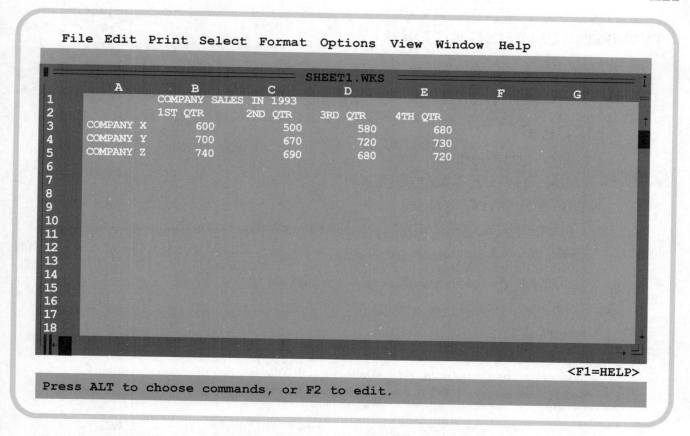

3 Save this spreadsheet by proceeding as follows:

Choose **File**

Choose **Save As**

Type **A:QUARTER** **<Return>**

4 Close this file by choosing **File** and **Close**

EXAMPLE 2: CREATING A GRAPH

Using the QUARTER file, produce a graph of the sales in each quarter for Company X.

METHOD

1 Load the QUARTER file:

   Choose **File** and **Open Existing File**

   Type **A:QUARTER <Return>**

2 Select the cells B2 down to E3. These cells contain the Quarters and Sales in Company X only.

   (Select the range of cells *either* by clicking the mouse on B2 and then keeping the mouse button down while moving the arrow down to E3, *or* by moving the highlight to B2, choosing **Select** and **Cells** then moving the highlight down to E3.)

   The required range B2 to E3 is now highlighted.

3 Choose **View**

   Choose **New Chart**

   The screen changes and the graph produced is displayed on your screen as shown below:

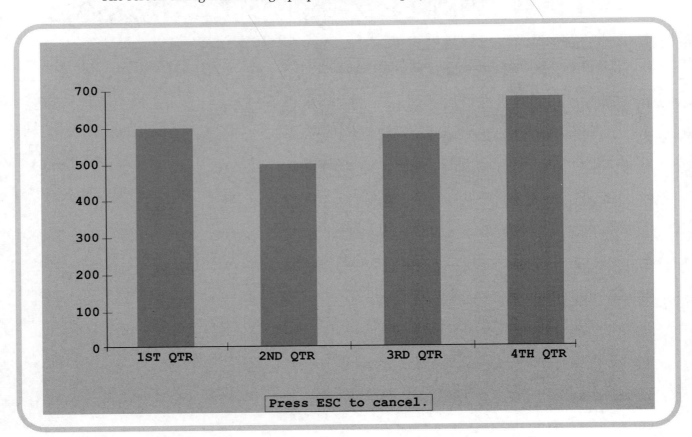

This graph compares the sales in each quarter for Company X.

4 Press **<Esc>** to return to the spreadsheet.

EXAMPLE 3: AMENDING A GRAPH

Incorporate information on the other companies' sales in each quarter, within the graph.

In order to do this we need to change the range of data we have selected.

METHOD

1 Select the range of cells from B2 down to E5. (This should be done by highlighting the required range as shown in Example 2. If you are not using a mouse, choose **View** and **Spreadsheet** before doing this.)

This range includes the four quarters' sales figures for the three companies.

2 Choose **View**

Choose **New Chart**

You will see that three bars are illustrated for each quarter. Each bar represents sales for a different company.

3 Press **<Esc>** to display the spreadsheet.

4 Choose **File** and **Save**

The spreadsheet together with the graphs have been saved in the QUARTER file.

Any time you retrieve QUARTER you will automatically be able to look at these graphs.

EXAMPLE 4: INCORPORATING LEGENDS

Change the graph again to include a legend (or key) to indicate what each bar represents.

The QUARTER file should be loaded and the spreadsheet displayed on your screen.

METHOD

1 Choose **View** and **Spreadsheet**

2 Select the range of data from A2 down to E5.

These cells not only include the headings for each quarter but also the labels for each set of data (i.e. each company). Each label will be displayed as a Legend (or Key).

3 The range A2 to E5 will now be highlighted.

Choose **View**

Choose **New Chart**

The graph will now be displayed including the legend as shown below:

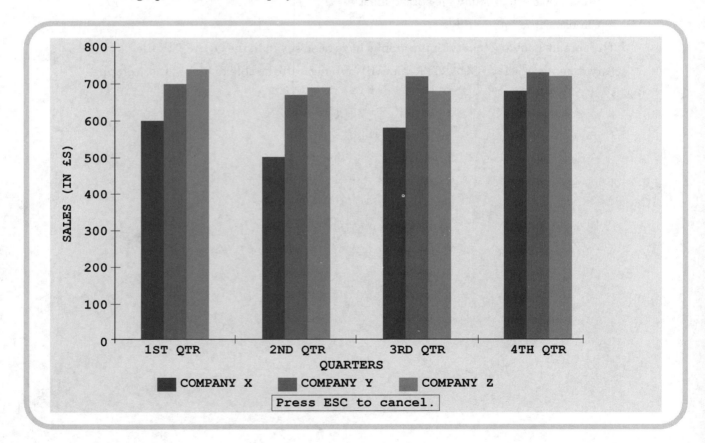

4 Press **<Esc>** to display the spreadsheet.

5 Choose **File** and **Save** to save the spreadsheet.

EXAMPLE 5: INCORPORATING TITLES

Insert titles into the graph created in the previous example.

METHOD

1 The spreadsheet should be displayed with the chart options at the top of the screen. To ensure this proceed as follows:

Choose **View**

Choose the latest chart; e.g. **Chart 3**

2 Press **<Esc>**

Choose **Data** then **Titles**

Type **COMPANY SALES IN 1993** (Do *not* press **<Return>**)

3 Move the cursor down to the X-axis line by pressing **<Tab>** or by using the mouse.

Type **QUARTERS** (do *not* press **<Return>**). Now move dow n to the Y-Axis line.

Type **SALES (IN £s)**

Press **<Return>** or click on **<OK>**

4 Now choose **View**

5 Choose the latest chart: e.g. **Chart 3**

The titles will now be placed on the graph as shown below.

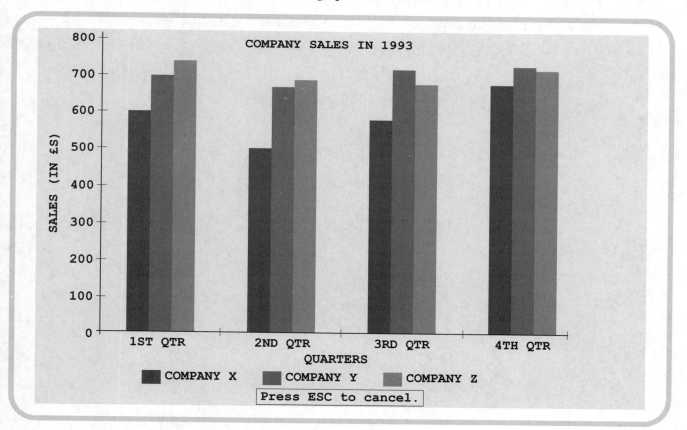

6 Press **<Esc>** to display the spreadsheet.

7 Choose **File** and **Save**

The latest graph has been saved with your spreadsheet.

EXAMPLE 6: CHANGING THE GRAPH TYPE

Experiment with displaying the graph (from Example 5) in different graph types.

METHOD

1 The QUARTER file should be loaded.

   View the latest graph (Chart 3) and then press **<Esc>**

2 Choose **Format**

3 You now see a list of different graph types available.

   Choose **Stacked Bar**

4 Choose **View**

   Choose the latest graph: e.g. **Chart 3**

   You will see that the bars are now *stacked* on top of each other instead of separately.

5 Press **<Esc>**

   Choose **Format**

   Choose **Line**

6 Now view the graph.

   You will see that each set of data is represented by a *line* instead of a bar.

7 Experiment with other graph types.

   Note that a pie chart only illustrates the first set of data (e.g. the first company).

EXAMPLE 7: PRINTING OUT GRAPHS

Print out a graph you have set up in a previous example.

Ensure that the spreadsheet is loaded.

METHOD

1 View the graph.

2 Press **\<Esc\>** to return to the spreadsheet.

   Choose `Print`

   Choose `Print`

   Press **\<Return\>** or choose `Print`

3 Printing a graph takes quite a long time. At the bottom left hand corner of your screen you are given an update of the percentage of the graph that has already been sent to the printer. When this reaches 100% you will obtain a print-out of the selected graph.

NOTES

You can preview the print-out of your graph by choosing `Print` and then `Preview`. This will enable you to print out the final version of your graph only.

TEST

1 Produce a spreadsheet containing the following information (*Note*: it is advisable not to leave any blank rows or columns between data if you intend to use the Chart facility.)

NUMBER OF STAFF LEAVERS

	Dept A	Dept B	Dept C	Dept D
January	23	12	35	27
February	17	10	31	19
March	5	9	19	20

2 Draw a graph to compare the number of staff leavers in each department over the three-month period.

3 Insert appropriate titles for this graph and save the spreadsheet as LEAVER.

4 Obtain a preview and then print out this graph.

FURTHER EXERCISES

1 i)   Create a spreadsheet containing the following information on monthly costs:

	January	February	March	April
Housing	600	650	650	670
Travel	100	110	105	115
Food	220	190	250	240
Services	120	95	130	150

   ii) Draw a line graph of the housing expenses over the four-month period.
   iii) Use a stacked bar graph to illustrate all the expenses over the four-month period and print out this graph.
   iv) Insert some costs for May into the spreadsheet and incorporate these values in the graph.

2 i)   Use the DEPT2 file (created in Lesson 4) to produce a graph of the gross profit obtained for each of the five departments.
   ii) Incorporate information on the costs in each department within the graph you have produced.
   iii) Ensure that you have labels on the X-axis and that a legend is displayed.
   iv) You will see that gaps in your spreadsheet cause problems in the resulting graph. Edit the spreadsheet by removing any blank rows or columns and produce a new graph.
   v)   Place titles on this graph and print out the result.

You are now ready to go on to Lesson 6: Introduction to Databases.

Lesson 6:

INTRODUCTION TO DATABASES

In this session we will consider the basic database facilities available within Works. If you have not previously used databases, you should refer to the section headed 'Notes on Databases' on page 91 before proceeding with this lesson.

At the end of this lesson you will be able to:

- create a database
- add records to a file
- load an existing file
- list records in a file
- edit the contents of a file
- exit from the database package.

Load Works. The Works Main Menu will be displayed on your screen.

EXAMPLE 1: LOADING THE DATABASE PACKAGE

Load the Database package and display a blank file.

METHOD

1 Choose **File**

2 Choose **Create New File**

NOTE:

Options can be chosen in any one of three ways:
i) using the mouse, move the arrow to the required option and click the button;or
ii) using the arrow keys, move the highlight to the required option and press **<Return>** *or,*
iii) Type the highlighted letter of the required option: eg. **N** for **Create New File**

The screen will be displayed as shown at the top of the next page.

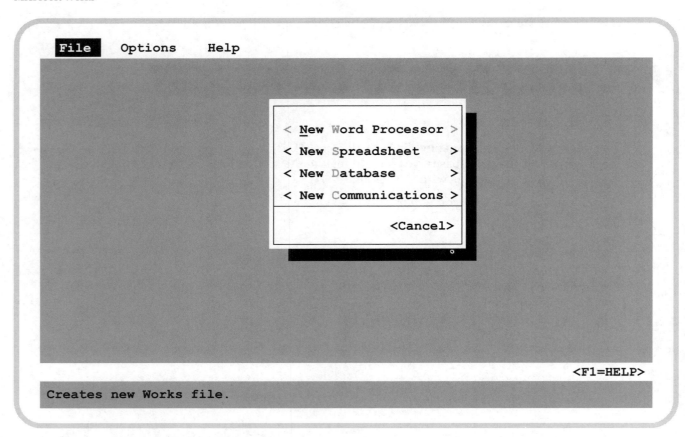

3 Choose **New Database**

(Either click on this option or type **D**).

4 A blank screen will be displayed with the main database options given at the top as shown in the following screen:

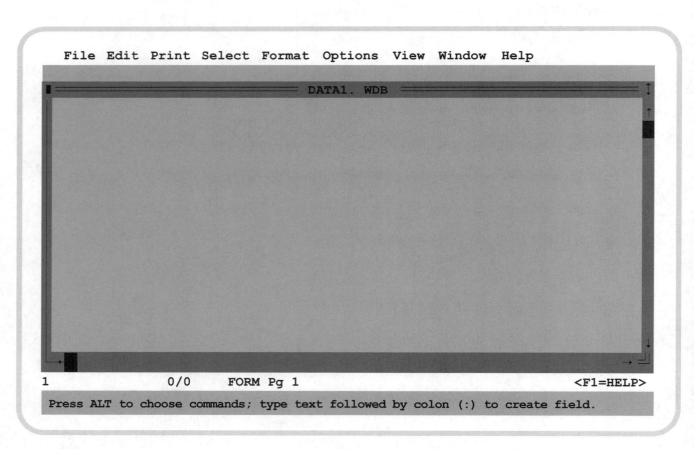

EXAMPLE 2: CREATING A DATABASE

Create a new file containing information on employees. The following details should be included in the file: employee's name, address and salary.

Ensure that a blank screen is displayed.

METHOD

1 Each piece of information will be saved in a separate field in the database. Each field is created by typing in the field name followed by a colon.

2 Move the cursor down a few lines (you can do this by either clicking the mouse in a new position, or using the arrow keys).

3 Type **NAME: <Return>** (Do not forget the colon!)

The following screen will be displayed:

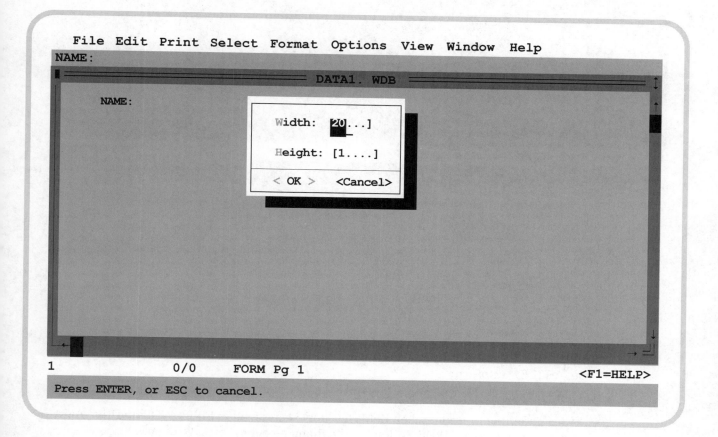

In this screen you can determine how much space is allocated for the information in a given field. The standard is 20 characters wide by one line.

4 Type **30 <Return>**

You will see that the NAME field has been specified together with the field width.

5 Move the cursor down two lines:

Type **ADDRESS: <Return>**

Type **35 <Return>**

The ADDRESS field has now been specified as being 35 characters wide.

6 Move the cursor down two lines:

Type **SALARY: <Return>**

Type **12 <Return>**

All the fields required for the employee file have now been specified. The screen will be displayed as shown below:

```
  File  Edit  Print  Select  Format  Options  View  Window  Help
┌──────────────────────────────────── DATA1. WDB ────────────────────────────────┐
│▌                                                                               ↑│
│                                                                                 │
│    NAME: . . . . . . . . . . . . . . . . . . . . . . . . . . . . . . . .        │
│                                                                                 │
│    ADDRESS: . . . . . . . . . . . . . . . . . . . . . . . . . . . . . .         │
│                                                                                 │
│    SALARY: . . . . . . . . . . . . . .                                          │
│                                                                                 │
│                                                                                ↓│
└─────────────────────────────────────────────────────────────────────────────→─┘
 1           0/0       FORM Pg 1                                        <F1=HELP>
 Press ALT to choose commands; type text followed by colon (:) to create field.
```

7 Now save this file by the following method:

Choose **File**

(Press **<Alt>** and then **F** or click on the **File** option.)

Choose **Save As**

(Type **A** or click on the **Save As** option.)

Type **A:FILE1 <Return>**

(Do *not* put spaces in a filename; e.g. FILE 1 is not an acceptable filename.)

The file containing information on fields has now been saved as FILE1.WDB on Drive A. (All database files will have .WDB following the filename when you save them.)

EXAMPLE 3: ADDING RECORDS

Using the file you have just created, add the details given below on four employees:

NAME	ADDRESS	SALARY
Harry Smith	1 The Hill	21000
Elizabeth Thomas	2 Myrtle Avenue	25500
George Ghana	34 The Lanes	23400
Jane Edwards	59 High Street	18450

METHOD

1 The screen should be displayed showing the blank fields you created in Example 2.

2 Move the cursor to the right of NAME:

The empty NAME field will now be highlighted.

Type **Harry Smith <Return>**

3 Now move the cursor down to the ADDRESS field (do this by clicking in the empty ADDRESS field or pressing **<Tab>**).

Type **1 The Hill <Return>**

4 Move down to the SALARY field.

Type **21000 <Return>**

5 Now we have inserted all the details for the first record.

Press **<Tab>** to display the next blank record.

6 Type **Elizabeth Thomas <Return>**

Move the cursor to the ADDRESS field.

Type **2 Myrtle Avenue <Return>**

Move the cursor to the SALARY field.

Type **25500 <Return>**

7 Press **<Tab>** to display the next blank record.

Type **George Ghana <Return>**

Press **<Tab>**

Type **34 The Lanes <Return>**

Press **<Tab>**

Type **23400 <Return>**

Press **<Tab>** for the next record.

8 Now insert the details for Jane Edwards into this blank record.

9 Save this file:

Choose **File**

(Press **<Alt>** then **F** or click on the **File** option.)

Choose **Save**

(Press **S** or click on **Save** .)

The four records you have inserted are now saved in the file called FILE1.WDB on Drive A.

EXAMPLE 4: FINISHING IN THE DATABASE PACKAGE

Exit from the database package.

METHOD

1 Choose   File

2 Choose   Close

(If you have made any changes to the file since saving you will be asked whether you wish to save these changes. Just choose   Yes   or   No)

The Works Main Menu is now displayed and the screen has been cleared of the file you have set up.

EXAMPLE 5: LOADING A DATABASE FILE

Load the FILE1 database you created earlier.

The WORKS Main Menu should be displayed on screen.

METHOD

1 Choose **File**

  Choose **Open Existing File**

2 Type **A:FILE1 <Return>**

The file has now been loaded, and a single record is displayed on your screen.

EXAMPLE 6: LISTING RECORDS

List all the records in the FILE1 file.

You can look at records in the file in two ways:

METHOD A: WITHIN ONE RECORD

1 Use **<Ctrl>** together with **<Page Up>** or **<Page Down>** to move between records.

For example, pressing **<Ctrl>** and **<Page Up>** will take you to the previous record.

2 Look at all four records using this approach.

METHOD B: AT ALL THE RECORDS

1 Use **<Ctrl>** and **<Page Up>** to display the first record (e.g. Harry Smith).

2 Choose **View**

3 Choose **List**

All the records are now displayed as shown in the following screen:

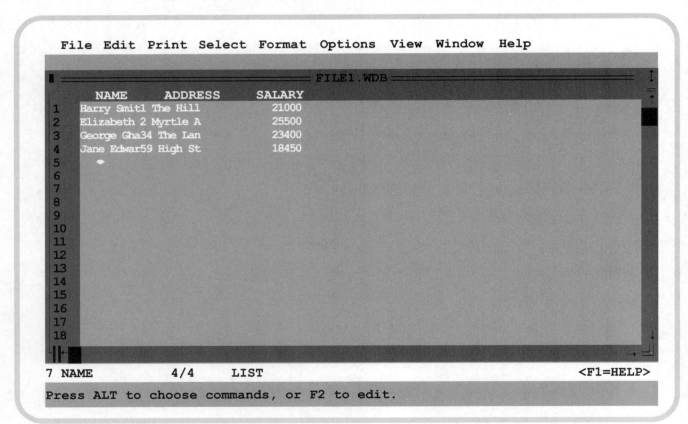

4 Each line displays a record. Only the first few characters in each field are displayed.

5 To be able to see all of the contents in each field, you must change the column widths for viewing.

Move to the NAME column: e.g. on 'Harry'.

Choose **Format**

(Click on **Format** or press **<Alt>** and **T**).

The following screen will be displayed:

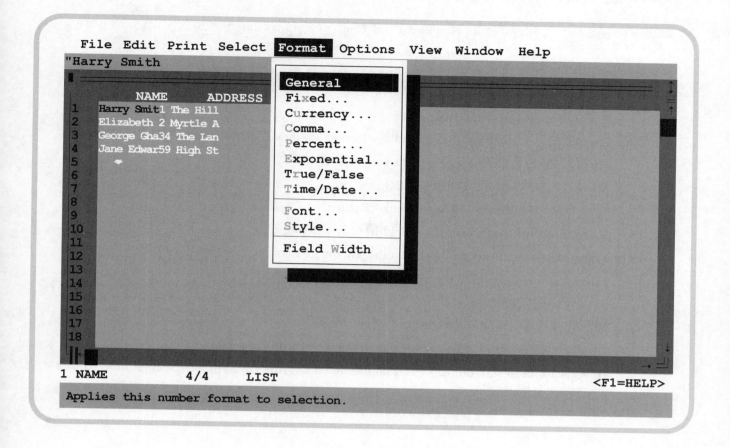

6 Choose **Field Width**

Type **20 \<Return\>**

The NAME column has now been widened.

7 Other field widths can be changed in the same way.

Move the cursor to the ADDRESS column: e.g. on '1 The Hill'.

Choose **Format**

Choose **Field Width**

Type **30 \<Return\>**

All the records will now be fully displayed.

8 Choose **View**

Choose **Form**

This will now take you back to the screen displaying a single record (or form).

EXAMPLE 7: EDITING RECORDS

Change Harry Smith's address to '46 New Road' and George Ghana's salary to £26,000.

METHOD

1 A single record should be displayed.

   Use **<Ctrl>** and **<Page Up>** or **<Page Down>** to move between records.

   Display Harry Smith's record on the screen.

2 Move the cursor to the ADDRESS field.

   Type the new address: **46 New Road <Return>**

   As soon as you start typing the old address is deleted.

3 Press **<Ctrl>** and **<Page Down>** until you locate George Ghana's record.

   Move the cursor down to the SALARY field.

   Type **26000 <Return>**

4 You have now edited the records.

   Choose **View** and **List** to look at all the records on the screen.

   (If you cannot see all four records then use the 'up' arrow key to move the cursor up. All the records will be displayed).

5 Now save these changes:

   Choose **File**

   Choose **Save**

6 Choose **File** and **Close** to exit from the database package and display the Main Menu.

TEST

1 Ensure that the database facility is loaded.

2 Create a new database file containing the following fields:

SURNAME	20 characters
SALARY	10 characters
DATE JOINED	10 characters
QUALIFIED	3 characters

3 Insert the following information:

SURNAME	SALARY	DATE JOINED	QUALIFIED
Barker	22000	20/11/90	Yes
Robertson	16000	16/03/86	No
James	19750	04/12/91	Yes
Smith	18400	23/05/89	Yes
Smith	24200	18/02/88	No

4 Display a list of these records on the screen.

5 Change James' salary to £22000.

6 Save this file as EMP1 and exit from Works.

FURTHER EXERCISES

1 i) Create a new file giving information on properties for sale in an Estate Agent's. The file will contain the following fields:

ADDRESS	40 characters
TYPE	10 characters
PRICE	10 characters

ii) Insert the following records into this file:

ADDRESS	TYPE	PRICE
34 High Street	House	106000
209 Myrtle Road	House	250000
37 Tree Lane	Bungalow	120000
3 Redwood Avenue	Flat	79500
88 Mill Lane	House	135000

iii) Display all these records on a single screen and ensure that the full details can be seen.

iv) Save this as a file called 'PROPERTY' and then exit.

2 i) Create a new file containing information on Hospital patients. The file will contain the following records:

NAME	SEX	ADMITTED	DOCTOR	OPERATION
Smith	M	20/05/92	Khan	Yes
Roskoff	F	11/06/92	Hunter	No
Arafat	M	09/06/92	Khan	No
Timms	M	16/06/92	Jones	Yes
Knott	F	20/06/92	Hunter	Yes

ii) Display these records on screen.

iii) Change the following information:

a) Roskoff's doctor is now a woman named Redman
b) Knott does not require an operation.

iv) Save this file as PATIENT and then exit.

You are now ready to go on to Lesson 7: Further Databases.

FURTHER DATABASES

In this session we will consider some additional features available using databases in Works.

At the end of this lesson you will be able to:

- Insert and delete records
- print out records
- locate specific records
- perform complex searches
- sort the file
- alter the format of the fields.

Load Works. The Works Main Menu will be displayed on your screen.

EXAMPLE 1: INSERTING AND DELETING RECORDS

Using the FILE1 file created in Lesson 6, delete Jane Edwards and insert two new employees before Elizabeth Thomas.

Use the following details for the two new employees:

NAME	ADDRESS	SALARY
Fred Mobullo	106 Freeway Drive	16000
Tracey Arlott	78 Cancun Way	19750

METHOD

1 Choose `File`

   Choose `Open Existing File`

   Type **A:FILE1 <Return>**

   The database is now loaded and a single record is displayed.

   (If all the records are displayed, choose `View` and `Form` to display a single record.)

2 We wish to delete Jane Edwards:

   Use the **<Ctrl>** and **<Page Up>** or **<Page Down>** keys to move between records and display the record on Jane Edwards.

   Now choose `Edit`

   Choose `Delete Record`

   The record previously displayed has now been deleted.

3 To check this, choose `View` and `List`

   Use the 'up' arrow key to display other records.

   There should now only be three records contained in this file.

4 We wish to insert records in front of Elizabeth Thomas:

Place the cursor on Elizabeth Thomas' record.

Choose **View** and **Form**

The record containing Elizabeth Thomas is now displayed.

5 Choose **Edit**

Choose **Insert Record**

A blank record is now displayed.

Move the cursor to the empty NAME field:

Type in **Fred Mobullo <Return>**

Press **<Tab>** to move into the next field.

Type **106 Freeway Drive <Return>**

Press **<Tab>**

Type **16000 <Return>**

6 Now insert another record:

Choose **Edit** and **Insert Record**

Type in the details on Tracey Arlott pressing **<Tab>** to move between fields.

7 To list all the records:

Choose **View** and **List**

You will now see that the two new records have been inserted into the file in the required position.

8 Save these changes:

Choose **File** and **Save**

These changes have now been saved on to FILE1 on Drive A.

EXAMPLE 2: PRINTING ALL RECORDS

Print out all the records in the FILE1 file.

There are two ways of printing records.

METHOD A

1 The FILE1 file should be loaded and a single record displayed on the screen.

(If all the records are currently displayed, choose **View** and **Form** to show a single record.)

2 Choose **Print**

Choose **Print**

The following screen is displayed, showing a number of print options:

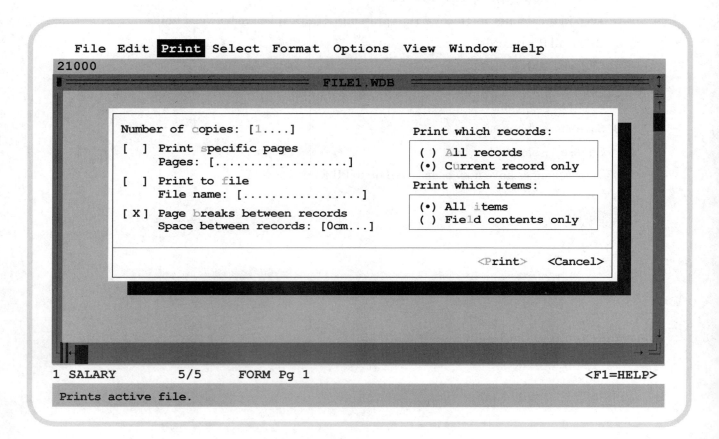

3 We wish to print All Records:

Choose **All Records**

(Do this by clicking on this option or moving the cursor into the required box using the **<Tab>** and arrow keys.)

4 Now choose **Print**

(click on **<Print>** or type **P**)

A print is now obtained of all the records in the file. Each record is printed on a separate page.

METHOD B

1 Choose **View** and **List**

All the records are shown.

2 Choose **Print**

3 Choose **Print**

Press **\<Return\>** or click on   **\<Print\>**

A print-out will now be obtained showing all the records on one page, one record per line.

(If all the columns cannot be printed on a single page they will appear on subsequent pages.)

EXAMPLE 3: SEARCHING A FILE

Display Fred Mobullo's record from the FILE1 file.

METHOD

1 We can search for specific records if the screen is displaying either a list of records or a single record (form).

In this example, display a single record:

Choose **View** and **Form**

2 Choose **Select**

The following screen will be displayed:

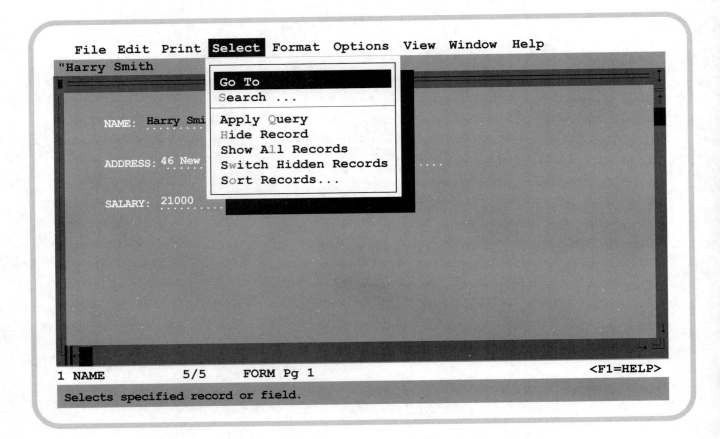

3 Choose **Search**

Type **Mobullo <Return>**

Fred Mobullo's record is automatically displayed on screen.

4 Experiment with this facility by searching for 'Road' or '25500'.

Do this while you have all the records listed on screen (using View and List).

You will see that the Search facility moves the cursor to the next record satisfying the given condition.

EXAMPLE 4: CARRYING OUT COMPLEX SEARCHES

Find all the employees earning more than £20,000.

METHOD

1 Choose **View** and **List** to display all the records on screen.

2 Choose **View**

Choose **Query**

3 Move the cursor to the empty SALARY field.

Type **>20000 <Return>**

4 Choose **View** and **List**

All the records listed satisfy the condition (salary >20000).

These selected records could now be saved in a separate file or printed out.

5 To return to the original list of records, you must delete the Query you have just created:

Choose **View** and **Query**

Choose **Edit**

Choose **Delete Query**

6 Now select **View** and **List**

All the records will now be displayed.

EXAMPLE 5: SORTING A FILE

Sort the employees into alphabetical order in FILE1.

FILE1 should be loaded and a single record (form) should be displayed on screen.

METHOD

1 Choose `Select`

Choose `Sort Records`

You can change the options displayed here if you need to.

The first field shows NAME. (If not, type **NAME**)

Choose `<OK>` or press `<Return>`

The records are now sorted into alphabetical order of name.

2 Choose `View` and `List`

Notice that the names are now in order: Elizabeth before Fred, Fred before George, etc.

3 Try the Sort facility again by sorting the employees in order of salary:

With all the records listed on screen:

Choose `Select`

Choose `Sort Records`

Type **SALARY** `<Return>`

The screen now displays all the employees in order of salary.

4 Choose `File` and `Save`

This file has now been re-saved as FILE1 on Drive A.

EXAMPLE 6: ALTERING THE FILE FORMAT

Using the FILE1 file, increase the width of the ADDRESS field to 40 characters and change the format of the SALARY field to Currency.

The FILE1 file should be loaded and a single record displayed on screen.

METHOD

1 Move the cursor to the ADDRESS field.

Choose **Format**

Choose **Field Width**

Type **40 <Return>**

The field width has automatically been increased.

2 Move the cursor to the SALARY field.

Choose **Format**

Choose **Currency**

Press **<Return>** to accept 2 decimal places.

Notice that the salary is now expressed in Currency format. (The figure is preceded by a £ sign.)

3 Choose **View** and **List**

Now that the figures are in a Currency format, they no longer fit into the SALARY column. Hence a series of £ £ £ are displayed.

Change the width of this column:

Move the highlight to anywhere in the SALARY column.

Choose **Format**

Choose **Field Width**

Type **15 <Return>**

The width has now been increased enough to enable the display of the salaries.

Move the cursor over to the SALARY column if these are not shown.

4 Choose **File** and **Save**

The file has now been re-saved as FILE1.

TEST

1 Close the current file and return to the Main Menu.

2 Load the EMP1 file from your disk. (This was created in the test at the end of Lesson 6. If you have not completed this, you will need to create the EMP1 file now in order to continue with this test.)

3 Sort the records into order of surname and print out the sorted file, one record per page.

4 List all the records that have a 'Yes' in the QUALIFIED field.

5 Change the SALARY field to a Currency format and ensure that the column width is large enough to list all records on the screen.

6 Delete Robertson's record and print out all the records with one record per line.

FURTHER EXERCISES

1 i) Create a new file containing details on shipping arriving into a dockyard. This file will contain the following fields:

NAME	30 characters
ORIGIN	20 characters
TONNAGE	8 characters
REGISTER	10 characters
CARGO	20 characters

ii) Insert the following records into this file:

NAME	ORIGIN	TONNAGE	REGISTER	CARGO
SS Hercules	Greece	50,000	20/11/89	Fruit
Armada	France	120,000	18/6/91	Steel
Lioness	Panama	75,000	21/7/90	Coal
Superior	Australia	154,000	30/9/92	Electrical
Ranger	Germany	90,000	3/3/86	Coal
Montego	Mexico	110,000	4/7/89	Fruit

iii) Change the REGISTER field to a Date/Time format.

iv) Display all the ships with a tonnage over 100,000.

v) Display all those ships registered before 1 Jan 1991. (Use <'1/1/91' in a Query.)

vi) Save the file as SHIP.

2 i) Load a file called PATIENT. (This file was created in Exercise 2 at the end of Lesson 6. If you did not complete this exercise, you will need to create the file now.)

ii) Add the following records into the file:

NAME	SEX	ADMITTED	DOCTOR	OPERATION
Ali	F	28/06/92	Khan	Yes
Jones	M	29/06/92	Hunter	No
Robertson	M	26/06/92	Jones	Yes

iii) Ensure that the ADMITTED field is in Date format, then list all those patients admitted after 15 June 1992.

iv) Sort the records in name order and print them out.

v) Print out all the females who require an operation.

You are now ready to go on to Lesson 8: Integrating Files.

Lesson 8:

INTEGRATING FILES

In this session we will deal with the process of integrating files created from the separate packages (word processing, spreadsheet and database) within Works.

At the end of this lesson you will be able to:

- open many files simultaneously
- move between files
- combine sections of files together
- create standard documents
- print mail-merged documents.

Load Works. The Works Main Menu will be displayed on your screen.

EXAMPLE 1: USING SEVERAL FILES TOGETHER

Display a number of files on the screen simultaneously.

Any previous file should be closed before starting this example.

METHOD

1   Load in the INTRO file from the word processing program:

Choose   **File**

Choose   **Open Existing File**

Type   **A:INTRO   <Return>**

INTRO.WPS is now displayed on your screen.

2   Similarly, without closing any file, load other files such as the following:

A:SALES (spreadsheet)
A:FILE1 (database).

3   Three files are now currently open and are stacked up. You may be able to see the edge of each display as shown at the top of the next page.

```
  File  Edit  Print  Select  Format  Options  View  Window  Help
┌──────────────────────────── INTRO.WPS ─────────────────────────────┐
│                        ┌───────── SALES.WKS ──────────┐             │
│                        │    ┌──────── FILE1.WDB ───────────────┐    │
│  1                     │  NAME              ADDRESS        SALARY│    │
│  2  │1   Fred Mobullo      106 Freeway Drive       £16,000.00 │    │
│  3  │2   Tracey Arlott     78 Cancun Way           £19,750.00 │    │
│  4  │3   Harry Smith       46 New Road             £21,000.00 │    │
│  5  │4   Elizabeth Thomas  2 Myrtle Avenue         £25,500.00 │    │
│  6  │5   George Ghana      34 The Lanes            £26,000.00 │    │
│  7  │6                                                        │    │
│  8  │7                                                        │    │
│  9  │8                                                        │    │
│ 10  │9                                                        │    │
│ 11  │10                                                       │    │
│ 12  │11                                                       │    │
│ 13  │12                                                       │    │
│ 14  │13                                                       │    │
│ 15  │14                                                       │    │
│ 16  │15                                                       │    │
│ 17  │16                                                       │    │
└─────┴─────────────────────────────────────────────────────────────┘
 7 SALARY        5/5     LIST                              <F1=HELP>
 Press ALT to choose commands, or F2 to edit.
```

FILE1 (the last file you opened) is displayed fully with the other files (SALES and INTRO) stacked behind. You may not be able to see all three columns (containing NAME, ADDRESS and SALARY), depending on the field width you have previously set.

4 You can now display any of these files by switching between windows:

Choose **Window**

Choose **SALES.WKS**

The SALES spreadsheet is now displayed.

5 Using the Windows option will allow you to change between one file and another.

Display the FILE1 file on your screen again using the **Window** option.

6 Now, to display all the files on the screen:

Choose **Window**

Choose **Arrange All**

All three files are now displayed on the screen as shown on the next page.

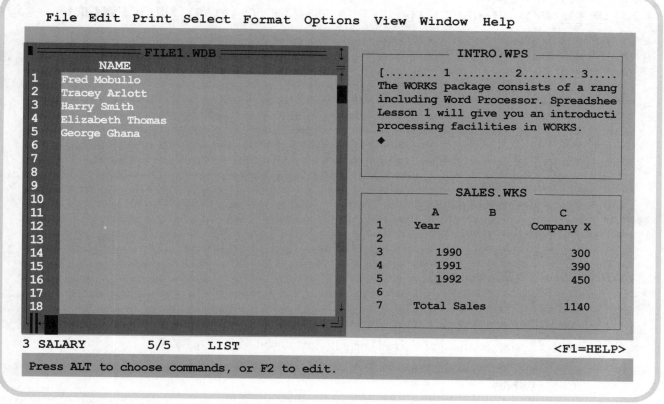

```
  File  Edit  Print  Select  Format  Options  View  Window  Help

  ┌───────────────── FILE1.WDB ─────────────────┐    ┌───────── INTRO.WPS ─────────┐
  │        NAME                                  │    │ [......... 1 ......... 2......... 3.....│
  │ 1   Fred Mobullo                             │    │ The WORKS package consists of a rang│
  │ 2   Tracey Arlott                            │    │ including Word Processor. Spreadshee│
  │ 3   Harry Smith                              │    │ Lesson 1 will give you an introducti│
  │ 4   Elizabeth Thomas                         │    │ processing facilities in WORKS.     │
  │ 5   George Ghana                             │    │ ◆                                   │
  │ 6                                            │    └─────────────────────────────┘
  │ 7                                            │
  │ 8                                            │    ┌───────── SALES.WKS ─────────┐
  │ 9                                            │    │          A        B        C        │
  │ 10                                           │    │ 1   Year                Company X   │
  │ 11                                           │    │ 2                                   │
  │ 12                                           │    │ 3     1990              300         │
  │ 13                                           │    │ 4     1991              390         │
  │ 14                                           │    │ 5     1992              450         │
  │ 15                                           │    │ 6                                   │
  │ 16                                           │    │ 7   Total Sales         1140        │
  │ 17                                           │    │                                     │
  │ 18                                           │    └─────────────────────────────┘
  └──────────────────────────────────────────────┘

  3 SALARY        5/5      LIST                                      <F1=HELP>
  ┌────────────────────────────────────────────────────────────────────────┐
  │ Press ALT to choose commands, or F2 to edit.                           │
  └────────────────────────────────────────────────────────────────────────┘
```

FILE1.WDB is highlighted, showing that this is the file currently being used.

7   Within the current window you can use the arrow keys to move the cursor around. Alternatively, using the mouse, you can click on the arrows situated at the bottom and right of the current window.

Try clicking on the right arrow situated at the bottom right-hand corner of the current window. By doing this you will move across the window enabling other details in the file to be viewed.

8   To move between windows:

either Click an arrow on the window required

or   Choose **Window** and select the required file.

The new window is now made current and you can move around in this file as usual.

9   The current window can be expanded to fill the screen by doing one of the following:

either Click on the double arrow symbol situated at the top right-hand corner of the current window

or   Choose **Window** then
          Choose **Maximise**

Repeating this procedure will return you to the original split screen.

10 Experiment with moving between windows and displaying the current window as a full screen.

11 Finally, close all the files currently displayed without saving any changes.

EXAMPLE 2: COMBINING FILES (SPREADSHEET TO WORD PROCESSOR)

Incorporate a spreadsheet into a word-processed file and print it out.

METHOD

1 Open up the INTRO file:

Choose **File**

Choose **Open Existing File**

Type **A:INTRO** **<Return>**

2 Open up the SALES file:

Choose **File**

Choose **Open Existing File**

Type **A:SALES** **<Return>**

3 We will incorporate part of this spreadsheet into the word-processed document.

Select a range on the spreadsheet currently displayed, e.g. A1 to E5. This range should now be highlighted.

Choose **Edit**

Choose **Copy**

This range has now been selected.

4 Move to the INTRO document:

Choose **Window**

Choose **INTRO.WPS**

The word-processed document is now displayed.

5 Move the cursor down to the position where you wish to insert the selected range. For example, move down to the bottom of this document.

6 Press **<Return>**

The part of the spreadsheet selected has now been inserted into the document.

(Note that each column in the spreadsheet is displayed at a new tab position in the word-processed document. Therefore, the tabs must be set *before* bringing a spreadsheet into a document.

7 Choose **Print**

Choose **Print**

Choose **<Print>** or press **<Return>**

The new document will now be printed.

8 Close these files without saving the changes.

NOTES

This example shows the standard approach to moving data from one file to another. Firstly, the two files should be opened. Next, select a range to be copied; then choose **Edit** and **Copy** . Finally, go to the new file and move the cursor to the required position before pressing **<Return>**

EXAMPLE 3: COMBINING FILES (CHARTS TO WORD PROCESSOR)

Incorporate a graph into a word-processed document.

We will open up a spreadsheet file where a chart has already been set up.

The QUARTER file made in Lesson 5 will be used for this purpose.

METHOD

1 Open up the word-processed document: e.g. A:INTRO.

2 Open up the spreadsheet file: e.g. A:QUARTER.

3 Display the word-processed document:

   Choose **Window**

   Choose **INTRO.WPS**

4 Now move the cursor to the position in your document where the graph is to be inserted.

   Choose **Edit**

   Choose **Insert Chart**

   The following screen will be displayed:

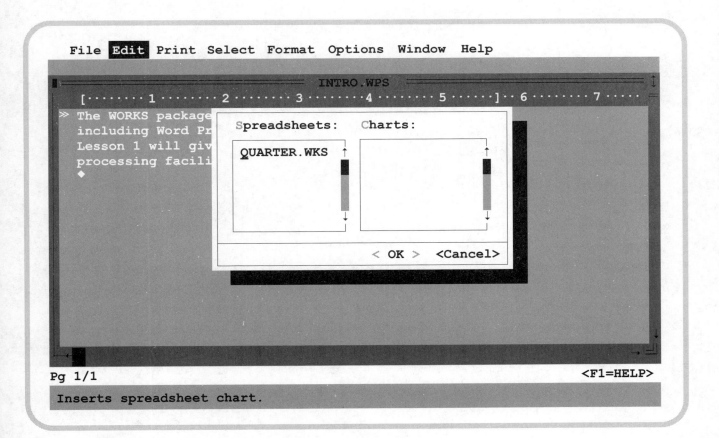

This screen displays the spreadsheets currently open.

5 Choose **QUARTER** (either click on QUARTER.WKS or press **<Space>**).

   A list of charts already created in this file are now displayed.

Choose a chart: e.g. **Chart 3**

Press **\<Return\>** or click **\<OK\>**

6 The chart has now been inserted into your document.

You will see the *name* of the chart specified on screen; such as

chart QUARTER.WKS:Chart3

The actual graph will not be displayed but will be reproduced when printed.

7 Print out this document as follows:

Choose **Print**

Choose **Print**

Choose **\<Print\>** or press **\<Return\>**

8 Graphs take a long time to print. A message will be displayed at the bottom of your screen:

Press Esc to cancel printing

This is shown whilst the document is being sent to the printer.

When complete the message will change to:

Press Alt to choose commands

The document (including the graph) will now be printed out.

EXAMPLE 4: MAILMERGING (DATABASE TO WORD PROCESSOR)

Using the FILE 1 database, create personalised memos to employees from the standard letter given below.

Memo to: <NAME>

Your new salary has been calculated to be <SALARY> per year.

In order to check our records could you please confirm whether the following address details are correct:

<ADDRESS>

Thank you for your cooperation.

Fred Brindisi

Personnel Manager

METHOD

1 Close all previous files and open the FILE1 database.

The database should be displayed showing NAME, ADDRESS and SALARY.

2 Use the word processor to create the memo document (given above) as follows:

Create a new word processor document and proceed as follows:

Type **Memo to:**

3 With the cursor at this point:

Choose **Edit**

Choose **Insert Field**

4 A list of databases is displayed: including FILE1.

Choose FILE1 (Click the mouse on **FILE1.WDB** or press **<Space>**)

5 A list of fields is displayed: e.g. NAME, ADDRESS and SALARY

Choose **NAME** (move the cursor to NAME and press **<Space>** or click on **NAME** .)

Press **<Return>** or click on **<OK>**

This is now inserted into your document and shown by **<<NAME>>**.

6 Continue to type the memo as shown:

Type **Your new salary is calculated to be**

7 Now, again you must select a field as shown:

Choose **Edit**

Choose **Insert Field**

Choose **FILE1.WDB** and the required field, e.g. SALARY

Press **<Return>** or click on **<OK>**

<<SALARY>> will now be inserted into your document.

8 Continue typing:

per year.

In order to check our records could you please confirm whether the following address details are correct:

9 Now choose the ADDRESS field:

Choose **Edit**

Choose **Insert Field**

Select **FILE1.WDB** and choose **ADDRESS**

Press **<Return>** or click **<OK>**

10 Complete the memo by typing:

Thank you for your cooperation.

Fred Brindisi
Personnel Manager

The screen will now appear as shown below:

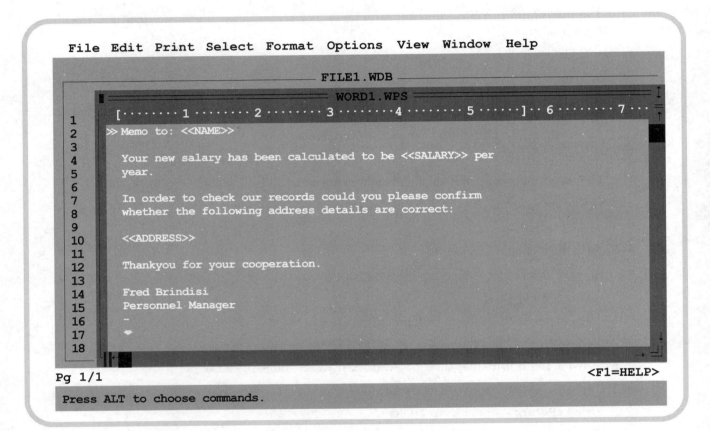

```
 File  Edit  Print  Select  Format  Options  View  Window  Help
                              FILE1.WDB
                             WORD1.WPS
       [ · · · · · · · 1 · · · · · · · 2 · · · · · · · 3 · · · · · · · 4 · · · · · · · 5 · · · · · · ] · 6 · · · · · · · 7 · · ·
   1
   2   >> Memo to: <<NAME>>
   3
   4     Your new salary has been calculated to be <<SALARY>> per
   5     year.
   6
   7     In order to check our records could you please confirm
   8     whether the following address details are correct:
   9
  10     <<ADDRESS>>
  11
  12     Thankyou for your cooperation.
  13
  14     Fred Brindisi
  15     Personnel Manager
  16     -
  17
  18
 Pg 1/1                                                          <F1=HELP>
 Press ALT to choose commands.
```

11 Now print out the personalised memos as follows:

Choose **Print**

Choose **Print Form Letters**

Select the associated database: e.g. **FILE1.WDB**

Choose **<Print>**

The personalised memos will now be printed.

12 Save the word-processed file:

Choose **File**

Choose **Save As**

Type **A:MEMO <Return>**

13 Close all files to exit.

TEST

1   Produce the following word-processed document:

>The WORKS package allows us to integrate files created in any of the components. For example, it is easy to include a graph into a document such as the following:
>
>Also, databases can be included in the document and lists displayed as shown below:

2   In the appropriate place in this document, include any graph you have previously created (after the second paragraph). Also, using Edit and Copy, include any database (after the third paragraph).

3   Print out the resulting document.

4   Save the file and exit.

FURTHER EXERCISES

1 i)   Create a database file containing customer details as shown below:

NAME	ITEM	COST
Mr Smith	cucumbers	£45
Ms Jones	letraset	£95.50
Miss Rahmad	paper	£125
Mr O'Leary	pens	£23

       Save this as CUSTOM.

  ii)   Produce a standard letter containing the following:

>Dear <NAME>
>
>We have received your order for <ITEM> to the value of <COST>. This will be processed as quickly as possible.
>
>Yours sincerely
>
>J Karnaugh
>
>Sales Director

  iii) Print out personalised letters to the four customers listed.

  iv) In order to keep track of the customers you have replied to, select all the records in the database and copy into the bottom of the document. Print out this *single* document.

2 i)   Take the information contained in CUSTOM (created in Question 1 above) and insert it into a blank spreadsheet.

  ii)   Change the width of each column in the spreadsheet so that all cells are fully displayed.

  iii) Produce a pie chart showing the amount spent on the four items in this list.

  iv) Write a report using the word processor containing just a few lines of text. Incorporate into this report both the spreadsheet and chart you have produced. Print out the resulting document.

This concludes the Microsoft Works course.

Further exercises are available in the next section to reinforce the work done throughout this course.

The final sections include details of the procedures used in this course together with additional facilities for experimentation.

ADDITIONAL EXERCISES IN WORKS

1 i) Produce the following menu and ensure that each line is centred and highlighted as shown:

THE BLUE FIG RESTAURANT

DINNER

Taramasalata
Prawn Cocktail
Whitebait

* * *

Cream of Mushroom Soup
Consommee

* * *

Roast Beef
Saddle of Lamb
Dover Sole

* * *

Selected Vegetables

* * *

Coffee

    ii) Insert items of your own choice into this menu.

    iii) Insert selected desserts after the main course, to include Profiteroles and Gateaux.

    iv) Print out the resulting document and save as BLUEFIG.

2 i) Create the following document, giving a list of competitors in a forthcoming gymnastics competition. Insert appropriate tab settings for the required columns.

Time	Competitors	Judges
9.30 am	Andrea Boguti Steve Harris Rick Wyman	R Burnham S Tracey
10.00 am	Ian Strange Sean O'Leary Topu Yan	B Blackley
10.30 am	Lesley Farnham	R Burnham

    ii) Delete Steve Harris from the 9.30 am session and insert Francis Mackay and Ravi Puri into the 10.30 am session.

    iii) Preview the document, print out two copies and save this file as COMP.

3 i) You wish wish to send personalised letters to some of your clients. Produce a standard letter containing the following:

Dear

Thank you for your instructions regarding the property at

We are in the process of preparing promotional material and will advertise this
        at a price of   .

I will inform you as soon as we receive any interest in the property.

Yours sincerely

    ii) Place your name at the bottom of this letter and today's date at the top. Save this document as AGENT1 and clear the screen.

    iii) Produce a database of clients' details giving the name, address of the property, type and price as shown at the top of the next page.

Mrs Whittle, 4 Hazel Close, bungalow, £97,000
Mr Burden, 26 Parish Court, house, £175,000
Mr Eaton, 423 Noble Road, flat, £86,000
Miss Gucci, 18 Pine Road, house, £215,000

iv) Save this file as VENDOR1.
v) Using the above standard letter and database, produce personalised letters to all the clients listed.
vi) Delete Mr Burden and Mr Eaton and insert:

Mrs Grist, 217 Elm Grove, house, £199,000

vii) Print out the personalised letters for the amended list.

4 The table below gives the gross profit (in £1000's) of four companies over a four-year period. (Negatives indicate a loss for the period.)

	1992	1993	1994	1995
Company W	2500	3700	4100	3900
Company X	3200	1900	140	-820
Company Y	4100	2050	3700	4350
Company Z	1150	1700	2500	4100

i) Set up this information on a spreadsheet.
ii) Set up an additional column in your spreadsheet giving the total profit gained in each company over the four-year period.
iii) Set up an extra row giving the average company profit in each year.
iv) Insert an extra two companies in your spreadsheet with the following profits:

Company S	900	110	1300	1150
Company T	1500	400	2200	350

Adjust the formulae already entered in your spreadsheet to accommodate these companies.
v) Print out this spreadsheet.
vi) Draw a bar chart of the profit obtained by Companies X, Y, and Z over the four-year period and print out your graph.

5 The table below gives information on a number of employees in your company.

Name	Salary	Years of Service
J SMITH	20000	10
A BARKER	16000	25
P ROBERTSON	21000	8
L GREGORY	26000	12
H WRIGHT	32000	30
P BROWN	19000	36

i) Set up this information in a spreadsheet.
ii) Pension and redundancy payments are calculated as follows:

Pension = Salary * Years of Service / 60

Redundancy Lump Sum = 3 * Pension

Set up extra columns in your spreadsheet to calculate the pension and redundancy payments for each employee and calculate the totals.
iii) Delete P Robertson from this list and insert two employees:

B GREEN	19500	20 years
C DUNLOP	22000	24 years

Re-calculate the pension and redundancy totals including these employees.
iv) Draw a pie graph of the salaries and print out this graph.

6 The table below gives the income and costs in a company in the four quarters of 1993.

Income Projection: ABC Company – 1993

	Jan–Mar	Apr–Jun	Jul–Sep	Oct–Dec
GROSS SALES	14000	15000	16000	24000
COSTS: SALARIES	2000	2000	2000	2000
RENT/RATES	600	600	600	600
ADVERTISING	1200	1400	1600	1700
INTEREST	1800	1900	1700	1100
PURCHASES	400	4200	4500	4800

i) Set up this table in a spreadsheet.
ii) Change the format to Currency and adjust the column widths to tidy up the display.
iii) Insert formulae to calculate the total costs and profit (Profit = Gross Sales − Total Costs) in each quarter during the year. Ensure that these values are also displayed in the correct format.
iv) Print out and save the speadsheet.
v) Draw a line graph of the profit figures and print out your graph.
vi) Incorporate this graph into a report produced on the word processor describing the changes in profit during the year.

7 i) Create a file of a bank's customers containing the following details:

SURNAME	15 characters
INITIALS	6 characters
TITLE	4 characters
NUMBER	10 characters
BALANCE	10 characters

ii) Insert the following records to this file:

Surname	Initials	Title	Number	Balance
Smith	RB	Mr	106243	2500
Jones	C	Miss	107413	1120
Brown	A	Ms	129740	50.25
Abdul	ST	Mr	148295	315.50
Smith	V	Dr	192111	1250.75
Rossini	DC	Ms	148293	860

iii) Obtain a print-out of these records.
iv) Sort the file into order of surname and initials and print out the sorted file.
v) Print out only those customers with a bank balance of over £1000.

8 i) Create a file of outstanding orders containing the following records:

Number	Supplier	Phone	Value	Date Sent	Received	Paid
A361	XYZ Suppliers	21984	300	19/11/91	Yes	Yes
A117	Smith Co	0705-11221	450	15/3/92	No	No
C219	ABC Goods	0202-4212	1250	7/5/91	Yes	Yes
B131	John Smith	21774	37	7/11/92	Yes	No
B277	ABC Goods	0202-4212	415	25/9/92	No	No
A014	XYZ Suppliers	21984	199	2/6/92	Yes	No
C290	Fred Jarvis	0449-3668	216	29/9/92	Yes	Yes

ii) Print out all these records.
iii) Display all those orders which have not been received.
iv) Print out all those orders which have been received but have not been paid.
v) Delete orders numbered A361 and C290 and print out the remaining records in order of number.
vi) Display all those orders sent after April 1992 with a value of over £300.
vii) Produce a standard letter to include the supplier's name, value of order and date sent, then print out personalised letters to all those suppliers where the order has been received.

FURTHER WORKS FACILITIES

This section provides a brief summary of some Works facilities not included in this introductory text. If you have completed this course, you should feel confident about exploring additional features contained within the Works package, and the following list will help you to do this.

The options are listed under the three main headings of word processing, spreadsheets and databases. However, you will see that many facilities are common to all these tools.

WORD PROCESSING

Commands		Effect
File	File Management	Enables you to perform file management tasks such as copying, deleting and renaming files
File	Exit Works	Exit from Works with or without saving
Edit	Undo	Change document back and ignore previous command
Edit	Copy	Copy selected text
Edit	Delete	Delete selected text
Print	Insert Page Break	Place a page break at cursor position
Select	Search	Search for specified text
Format	Borders	Place borders around selected text
Options	Check Spelling	Check text for spelling errors
Options	Thesaurus	Offer synonyms for selected word

SPREADSHEETS

Commands		Effect
Edit	Move	Move a selected range of cells
Edit	Fill Series	Insert a sequence of values into selected cells
Print	Set Print Area	Select a range of cells for printing
Print	Insert Page Break	Print a new page starting at the current cursor position
Select	Row/Column	Select a row or column at the cursor
Select	Go To	Go to a specified cell
Options	Freeze Titles	Fix on the screen rows above and columns to left of cursor
Options	Protect Data	Protect contents of cells so that they cannot be changed
Window	Split	Split the spreadsheet so that two views can be displayed

DATABASES

Commands		Effect
Edit	Move	Move selected data to a new position
Edit	Copy	Copy selected data
Edit	Clear	Delete selected data
Edit	Fieldname	Change fieldname at cursor position

`Select`	`Cells`	Select specified range
`Select`	`Record`	Select current record
`Select`	`Field`	Select current field
`Options`	`Protect Data`	Protect current records
`View`	`New Report`	Create and display a report

NOTES ON SPREADSHEETS

If you have not previously used a spreadsheet package it may be helpful to read the notes in this section. It is useful to know what a spreadsheet is and to be aware of the associated jargon.

WHAT IS A SPREADSHEET?

A spreadsheet is a table consisting of a number of rows and columns. Here is a blank spreadsheet:

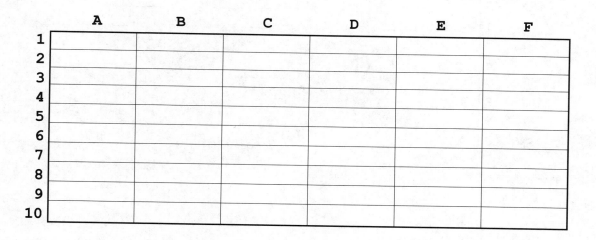

The *rows* and *columns* in this spreadsheet are labelled. Rows are numbered, and columns are labelled with letters.

CELLS

Using a spreadsheet is easy. Data (e.g. numbers or words) can be entered in any position (or cell) in the table. Each cell is referred to by a column letter and row number.

For example, the two cells B2 and E4 are illustrated in the next spreadsheet. (Note that the column letter is specified before the row number.)

RANGES

A group of cells together is called a *range*.

Ranges are defined by stating the cells in the top left-hand and bottom right-hand corners. For example, the range from B6 down to D8 would be referred to as B6:D8 as shown in the spreadsheet below:

	A	B	C	D	E	F
1						
2						
3						
4						
5						
6			B6:D8			
7						
8						
9						
10						

NOTES ON DATABASES

This section contains notes on databases which may be useful if you have not previously used a database package.

WHAT IS A DATABASE?

All information is contained in some type of *File*. A file contains a range of data, usually in a specific area. For instance, we have Personnel files, Customer files and Student files, all containing data for a particular group.

For example: Personnel files contain information on employees
Customer files may contain details of companies
Student files contain details on students.

These files can often be linked together, forming what is called a *database*. However, for the purposes of this introduction, you can think of a database as being the same as a file.

RECORDS

A file consists of a collection of *records*. Each record contains all the information on a single item in the file. For example, a single record in a Personnel file would contain all the details on a particular employee.

FIELDS

A record consists of a number of *fields*. Each field contains one specific piece of information within the record. For example, an employee record would contain details such as employee's name, address, salary and age. Each of these pieces of information would be contained in a separate field. The diagram below illustrates a sample file containing a number of such records.

	Field 1	Field 2	Field 3	Field 4
Record 1	Harry Wright	1 The High Street	£19,750	46 yrs
Record 2	Lisa Thomas	233 Mill Lane	£34,500	29 yrs
Record 3	Jake Mombassa	148 Brooks Lane	£23,000	37 yrs
Record 4	Elsie Tanton	45 Stanway Close	£12,000	59 yrs
Record 5	George Brazil	Swyre Farm Cottages	£15,000	21 yrs

USING A MOUSE TO LOOK AT THE SCREEN

When using a mouse, many of the basic procedures illustrated in this tutorial can be more easily achieved. The lessons in this book have included methods using either the mouse or keyboard. In this section we will consider extra ways of using the mouse in order to manipulate the screen. These will include the following prodecures:

- moving around the screen
- changing the window size
- splitting the window
- closing a file.

You can experiment with these facilities by creating some new files with nothing in them. If you have two or three files currently open, you will see the full benefit of using the procedures outlined below.

Many of the symbols you will see on a screen (or in a window) are the same whichever Works tool you are currently using. The screen below shows you some basic components of a typical window.

KEY TO DIAGRAM

A Click on this box to close file.

B Click on this double arrow to maximise the window size. Click again to return it to the original size.

C Click on this and 'drag' it to a new position to split the screen. This will enable you to look at different parts of a file at the same time.

D Click on these arrows to scroll around the document.

E Click and drag on these boxes to scroll much more quickly around the document. (Note: to 'drag', click on the symbol, keep the mouse button presed down and move the arrow to the new position.)

F This defines the bottom right-hand corner of the window. Click on this and drag to a new position to change the size of the window.

G Click and drag anywhere on this title bar to move the window to a new position on the screen.

H Click and drag anywhere on this border to move the window to the new position.

SUMMARY OF PROCEDURES

The following summary illustrates the procedures used in this tutorial pack.

The procedures are obtained from the menus within Works and can be obtained by either pressing the **<Alt>** key and then making the selection or using the mouse to click on the required option.

WORD PROCESSING

Lesson/Example	Commands		Effect
(1.1)	File	Create New File	Create a word-processed document
		New Word Processor	
(1.3)	File	Save	Save a document using current name and drive
(1.4)	File	Save As	Save a document using a new name/drive
(1.5)	File	Close	Close the current file
(1.6)	File	Open Existing File	Load an existing document
(1.7)	Format	Underline	Turn underline on
	Format	Plain Text	Turn highlighting off
	Format	Bold	Turn bold on
(1.8)	Print	Print	Print out the document
(1.9)	File	Exit Works	Exit from the package
(2.1)	Select	Text	Select a block of text for editing
(2.2)	Format	Centre	Centre selected text
(2.3)	Print	Preview	Look at how the document will be printed
(2.4)	Edit	Move	Move selected text to a new position
(2.5)	Select	Replace	Search for specified text and replace with new text

SPREADSHEETS

Lesson/Example	Commands		Effect
(3.1)	File	Create New File	Create a new spreadsheet file
		New Spreadsheet	
(3.3)	File	Save As	Save a spreadsheet using a specified filename
(3.4)	File	Close	Close the current file
(3.5)	File	Open Existing File	Load an existing spreadsheet
(3.7)	Print	Print	Print out the current spreadsheet
(4.1)	Edit	Insert Row/Column	Insert extra lines into the spreadsheet
(4.2)	Edit	Copy	Copy a cell or range of cells
(4.2)	Select	Cells	Highlight a range of cells
(4.3)	Edit	Fill Down	Copy down to a range of cells
(4.4)	Format	Currency	Format a range of cells to display as currency

	Format	Fixed	Format a range of cells to a fixed number of decimal places
(4.5)	Format	Column Width	Change column width of a range of cells
(4.6)	Print	Preview	Look at how the spreadsheet will be printed
	File	Save	Save a spreadsheet using the current name

CHARTS

Lesson/ Example	Commands		Effect
(5.2)	View	New Chart	Look at a newly created graph (chart)
(5.3)	File	Save	Save current spreadsheet together with all chart settings
(5.5)	Data	Titles	Insert titles into the current graph
	View	Charts	Look at a specified graph
(5.6)	Format	Stacked Bar	Choose a specified graph type (e.g. stacked bar graph)
	Format	Line	Choose a different graph type (e.g. line graph)
(5.7)	Print	Print	Print a graph after viewing

DATABASES

Lesson/ Example	Commands		Effect
(6.1)	File	Create New File New Database	Create a new database file
(6.2)	File	Save As	Save the database using a specified file name
(6.3)	File	Save	Save the database using the current file name
(6.4)	File	Close	Close the current file
(6.5)	File	Open Existing File	Load an existing database
(6.6)	View	List	Display all records
	Format	Field Width	Change the width of the current field
	View	Form	Display a single record on the screen
(7.1)	Edit	Delete Record	Delete the current record
	Edit	Insert Record	Insert a record in the current position
(7.2)	Print	Print	Print out the database
(7.3)	Select	Search	Search for specified details
(7.4)	View	Query	Set up a Query for searching the database
	Edit	Delete Query	Remove current Query
(7.5)	Select	Sort Records	Sort records into order
(7.6)	Format	Currency	Change display of numeric field

INTEGRATING FILES

Lesson/ Example	Commands	Effect
(8.1)	Window	Switch between windows

	Window	**Arrange All**	Display all the windows simultaneously
	Window	**Maximise**	Display the current window on full screen
(8.2)	**Edit**	**Copy**	Copy a selected range
(8.3)	**Edit**	**Insert Chart**	Insert a graph into a word-processed document
(8.4)	**Edit**	**Insert Field**	Insert a field marker in the current document
	Print	**Print Form Letters**	Produce personalised documents

GETTING OUT OF DIFFICULTIES

This section contains useful tips on sorting out problems which may occur when learning to use Works. If you encounter difficulties at any stage in this tutorial, ensure that you have followed the instructions precisely. If in doubt, go back to the beginning of the example. If you still have problems, the following points may be useful.

THE ESCAPE KEY

This key, usually labelled **<Esc>**, can be very useful for getting out of trouble. Pressing the Escape key will usually cancel what you are currently doing. If you have chosen an option on a menu, pressing **<Esc>** will take you back to the Main Menu. On some keyboards a **<Cancel>** option will be available. **<Cancel>** has the same effect as pressing **<Esc>**

OBTAINING HELP

The Works package offers a comprehensive Help facility. Help can be obtained in a number of ways: Press the **<F1>** key (or click on **<F1-Help>** , and you will see Help screens displayed that are relevant to what you are currently doing. Alternatively, choose **Help** and **Help Index** from the Main Menu displayed at the top of your screen. You can then choose the topic you need assistance on.

EDITING CELLS

When using a spreadsheet or database an entry can be edited in one of two ways: move the highlight to the cell you wish to edit and *either* type in the new data *or* press **<F2>** and then edit using the arrow keys, Delete and Backspace keys. When complete, press **<Return>**. The **<F2>** key is useful when you have a long or complicated entry to edit.

MOVING THE CURSOR

The arrow keys can be used to move the cursor around a document. The **<Page Up>** and **<Page Down>** keys can speed up the cursor movement. The mouse can also be used and provides a fast way of moving around in a document. Click on the mouse to move the cursor to the arrow position. (See also separate notes on using the mouse, page 92.)

SELECTING CELLS

In the spreadsheet and database facilities you will often need to select a range of cells. This can be done by one of the following:

i) using a mouse, click the button at the start of the range, then hold the button down whilst moving the arrow to highlight the required range; *or*

ii) Press **<Alt>** and then choose **Select** and **Cells** . Now move the cursor using the arrow keys, to highlight the required range.

Having selected the required range you can perform various functions such as editing, copying, deleting and printing.

ENTERING FORMULAE

When entering formulae into a spreadsheet you should always start with '='. The arithmetic operations (+ ,-, *, /) are performed in a certain order. Unless you are aware of this you may not get the required result! The order is as follows:

1 contents of brackets are calculated first
2 division (/) and multiplication (*) are then calculated
3 addition (+) and subtraction (-) are carried out last.

So, for example, C5+C6/2 will be calculated by dividing C6 by 2 and then adding C5. Alternatively, (C5+C6)/2 will be calculated by evaluating inside the brackets first, i.e. C5 added to C6, and then dividing the result by 2.

USING FUNCTIONS

There are many functions available in the Works spreadsheet or database facilities. The following is a selection of the more commonly used functions:

AVG   Average of values
MAX   Largest value in range
MIN   Smallest value in range
SUM   Total of values

For example, =AVG(B2:B12) will give the average of all values in cells B2 down to B12. Alternatively, in a database, =SUM(SALARY) will add up the SALARY fields. (Refer to the Works manual for more details on the use of functions.)

THE <ALT> KEY

This key is used to activate or de-activate a menu displayed at the top of the screen. If a menu is activated, *one* of the options is displayed in a block, and *all other options* have single letters highlighted. Once the menu is activated the options can be chosen as described below.

CHOOSING OPTIONS

Options can be chosen in a number of ways:

i) using a mouse, move the arrow on the screen to the required option and click the left button *or*
ii) press the **<Alt>** key to highlight the menu and either:
    a) move the highlight to the required option and press **<Return>** *or*
    b) press the highlighted letter of the required option.

If you do not see an option that is required in any of the examples ensure that you are using the correct View! For example, in database, using the options **View** **Form** or **View** **List** produces different sub-menus. Similarly, in spreadsheets, when viewing a spreadsheet or chart, you will see a different set of options on the menu.

THE ARROW KEYS

The arrow keys can be used to move the highlight or cursor around the screen. If your keyboard does not have separate arrow keys, you should find the arrows included in the numeric keypad to the right of the main keyboard. Ensure that the **<Num Lock>** is off, to enable the arrow keys to operate correctly.

In general, if available, it is easier to use the mouse when moving the cursor and/or choosing options.

SAVING

In Works you can usually save a file in one of two ways:

i) Use the **Save As** option. The package offers you a filename (e.g. WORD1, SHEET1, DATA1). Press **<Return>** or click **<OK>** to save using this name, or type in your own filename. The file will be saved on the current drive or directory. You can save to a different drive if you specify this with the filename, e.g. A:TEST will save a file called TEST on Drive A.

ii) Use the **Save** option. When saving a brand new file this has the same effect as the 'Save As' option. If you are re-saving an existing file this will save automatically, using the existing filename and directory.

LOADING FILES

You are able to load an existing file by using the **File** and **Open Existing File** option. You can then type in a filename. If you are loading a file that is not on the current drive or directory you must specify this with the filename. For example, typing A:FILE1 will then load FILE1 from Drive A.

If you have a number of files with the same name, it is advisable to use the extension as well. For example, if you have a word-processed file (SALES.WPS) and a spreadsheet (SALES.WKS) you should type in the full name required. For instance, if you type **A:SALES.WKS** you will retrieve the spreadsheet.

CHANGING THE CURRENT DRIVE/DIRECTORY

If you wish to change the current drive or directory, choose **File** and **Save As** . The current directory is displayed (e.g. Directory of C:/WORKS shows that we are currently using Drive C in the sub-directory WORKS). Alternative drives/directories are displayed in the Directories box. Using the mouse, click on the required directory and then on **<OK>** . A new current directory is
displayed. Now choose **<OK>** to save the file or **Cancel** to return to the menu. If you are not using the mouse, use the arrow keys to move to the required options.

PRINTING

If you have problems with printing any of the files produced in Works, check that the printer is connected to your computer and is set up correctly. The option **Print** includes a sub-option: **Printer Setup** . This will show you which printer you are currently set up to use (e.g. HPLaserjet) and which port you are using (e.g. LPT1). Check that these settings are correct. If in doubt, consult the Works manual.

The **Print** **Preview** option provides a useful way of looking at how your document will be printed.

GRAPHS (CHARTS)

Graphs can be difficult to set up and sometimes you may be surprised at the results. In general, if you select a range of cells to graph, the package separates this into the *minimum number of sets of data* regardless of rows or columns. For example, if you have selected 3 rows by 5 columns, you will obtain a graph of 3 sets of data, each containing 5 points. Alternatively, a range containing 6 rows and 2 columns will be graphed as two sets of data with 6 points in each set. To be more precise on specifying the data ranges you must use the **Data** option. This allows you to specify up to six sets of data (Y-series) and the labels for the x axis (X-series).